D0431773

WHETHER YOU'RE A SINGLE VEGETARIAN, an omnivore who's looking to incorporate more vegetables in your life, or a lone vegetarian in a meat-eating household, you know the frustrations of trying to shop, plan, and cook for one. How to scale back recipes? What to do with the leftovers from jumbo-sized packs of ingredients? How to use up all the produce from your farmer's market binge before it rots?

There's no need to succumb to the frozen veggie burger. With *Eat Your Vegetables*, award-winning food editor of *The Washington Post* and author of the popular column Cooking for One, Joe Yonan serves up a tasty book about the joys of solo vegetarian cooking. With 80 satisfying and globally-inspired vegetarian, vegan, and flexitarian recipes such as Spinach Enchiladas, Spicy Basil Tofu Fried Rice, and One-Peach Crisp with Cardamom and Honey, Yonan arms single vegetarians with easy and tasty meal options that get beyond the expected. In addition to Yonan's failproof recipes, *Eat Your Vegetables* offers practical information on shopping for, storing, and reusing ingredients, as well as essays on a multitude of meatless topics, including moving beyond mock meat and the evolution of vegetarian restaurants.

The perfect book for anyone looking to expand their vegetarian and produce-based repertoire, Yonan's charming, personable voice and unfussy cooking style encourage home cooks—both new and experienced—to take control in the kitchen and craft delicious veggie-centric meals for one.

# EAT YOUR VEGETABLES

# EAT YOUR VEGETABLES

## BOLD RECIPES FOR THE SINGLE COOK

NO LONGER PROPERTY OF
ANYTHINK LIBRARIES/
RANGEVIEW LIBRARY DISTRICT

# JOE YONAN

Photography by Matt Armendariz & Adam Pearson

**TEN SPEED PRESS**
Berkeley

For my sister Rebekah,
the first vegetarian I knew
and my favorite person
to cook with

# Contents

## Chapter 1
## SALADS and DRESSINGS

## Chapter 2
## SANDWICHES and SOUPS

Chapter 3

# BAKING, ROASTING, and BROILING

Chapter 4

# ON THE STOVETOP

# Preface

*I came to believe that since nobody else dared feed me as I wished to be fed,
I must do it myself, and with as much aplomb as I could muster.*

**—M. F. K. FISHER,** *An Alphabet for Gourmets,* **1949**

ONE OF MY obsessions in the 1980s was Bette Midler's comedy album, *Mud Will Be Flung Tonight,* and of all the tracks, my favorite is one in which she celebrates cynicism. In a singsong voice, accompanied by abstract plunking piano, she utters reason after reason to find the world disappointing—starting with the grandiose ("man's inhumanity to man") and descending into the picayune ("it's so hard to keep your ears clean")—followed by the same punch line, over and over: "Why bother?"

I mention it because "Why bother?" is the answer too many single people give when I ask what they cook for themselves for dinner. Their next remark is usually along the lines of "Why go to all that trouble if it's just me?" Sadly, they think the only time it's worth firing up the stove is when their cooking has an audience. I understand the impulse, but I have to say, there's really no such thing as *just* you. Who is more important? And if you live alone, as more and more of us do, it's silly, in my book, to think that every time you're hungry your only choices are takeout, a microwave pizza, or an impromptu dinner party. I love cooking for others, but plenty of nights I don't have any company, I'm enjoying my alone time, and I still want to eat—and eat well. I'm not going to lower my standards just because I'm the only one who is going to benefit

from the care I pour into my ingredients. I happen to think I—*just* I—am worth the bother.

Sure, there are obstacles. Single cooks have to overcome the challenges of shopping in supermarkets selling portions designed for families—or crowds. We have to come to terms with leftovers, a boon when they're in small quantities and an annoyance in large ones. But the advantages are formidable, too. At the top of my list: freedom. You don't have to take into account anyone's palate but your own, meaning you can let your cravings lead you where they may. The potential for satisfaction is huge.

That's why, several years ago, I started writing a column on cooking for one for the *Washington Post,* and that's why I wrote my first cookbook, *Serve Yourself: Nightly Adventures in Cooking for One,* in 2011. I wanted to proselytize about the joys of cooking for yourself, not apologize for it or bemoan the difficulties.

In promoting the book, I started noticing a phenomenon: at signings, classes, and festivals, a disproportionately high number of the single people who wanted to talk to me about my recipes were vegetarian or vegan. They wanted to know how much of the book would be suited to their way of eating. As I flipped through and pointed out all the dishes I thought they'd like (more than half of it is meatless), I started to realize something else: I was moving toward vegetarianism myself. It took me a little by surprise, especially since in the opening to that book's meat chapter, I had written: "The Texas boy in me, I'm afraid, would have a tough time ever giving meat up altogether. My connection to it is just plain hardwired."

The process has been organic, based not on one grand decision but on an evolution of my philosophy and my eating habits. And it hasn't felt like I'm giving anything up. Because of the environmental impact and horrid treatment of industrial livestock, I long ago started buying only humanely raised meat from small, local farms and tried to make it less of a focus on my plates. (The mantra is "less meat, better meat.") But less started to become *much* less. Phase one: I started noticing that my freezer was filling up with that meat, and I wasn't cooking it. Why not? Partly, I think, I was subconsciously trying to counter all the meat I was eating in restaurants. Phase two: I started getting less carnivorous at restaurants, too, finding that I was losing those Texas-boy cravings, little by little. Phase three: I started growing more of my own food in a community garden, then spent a year working on my sister and brother-in-law's homestead in Maine, just as they were deciding to become vegan. The modest bounty of my hard-won garden followed by the huge bounty of theirs gave me new inspiration for ways to cook vegetables. I might stay in this phase a good long while, or there might be a phase four. We'll see.

What set off this evolution? Health concerns have played a big part. I didn't have a heart attack; my doctor didn't tell me I needed to give up meat; there was no crisis per se. But the older I get, the more difficult it has become to manage my weight. And the older I get, the harder it is for my body to handle overly indulgent, multicourse tasting menu meals of pork belly, foie gras, sweetbreads, and lamb cheeks, the kinds of menus that in food-obsessed circles (like the ones I travel in) have gotten trendier and trendier. I just don't feel good after that kind of eating, and it takes me longer and longer to recover from these rich and meat-heavy meals.

Vegetables, on the other hand, invigorate me. From the moment I pluck them from the farmers' market display, dig them from the ground, or snip them from a plant, I'm imagining how I might cook them. And I love handling them. Stripping kale leaves from their stems, then swishing them around in the sink, grabbing them by the handful and stacking them on the countertop to be sliced can put me into a Zen state like no other. And the flavor! While it can take a little effort to coax it out of them, vegetables can run the gamut—bitter, tart, sweet, grassy—with all sorts of complexities layered within. They are lighter and brighter on the palate and in the stomach, which means that there is rarely a recovery period after a vegetable-focused meal. Instead, I'm usually filled with energy. I've said good-bye to those all-too-frequent food comas.

Still, I haven't banned meat from my diet altogether. I do consume small amounts of meat, poultry, and seafood here and there, either because it holds a particularly valuable cultural connection (turkey sausage or barbecued pork chops at one of my favorite barbecue stops on the drive home to West Texas), because I know just where it came from (my sister's Maine chickens, before we cleaned out the freezer and gave it all away), because a chef I know and respect works it into a dish in a way I'm curious to taste, or because I'm too polite to say no to a friend—or, God forbid, a friend's grandmother. But those experiences are getting fewer and farther between, and weeks and sometimes months go by without my consuming anything but fruits and vegetables, grains, beans, dairy, eggs, and maybe an anchovy or two for seasoning. I can't imagine that I will ever give up my milk, yogurt, eggs, and cheese, but that sounds an awful lot like what I said about meat just a couple of years ago. So who knows?

Vegetarianism, or the tendency toward it, has been growing slowly but surely in the United States, with 3 percent of adults calling themselves vegetarian in recent polls, and 8 percent saying they never eat meat. The fact is, there are compelling reasons for anyone to eat less meat or none at all. The connections between meat eating and risk of cancer, high blood pressure, and heart disease are well documented. When it comes to environmental issues, researchers point to the gases released through livestock production as having a bigger impact on climate change than all modes of transportation combined.

My impetus to write Eat Your Vegetables is simple: I want to help single cooks find as much inspiration in the garden, produce aisle, and farmers' market as I do. But I'm not here to tell anyone else how or what to eat. I bristle and look for the exit if I sense dogmatic, zealous, or fundamentalist attitudes, and I don't want to bring out that reaction in anybody else. That leaves me with a laissez-faire attitude toward other people's dietary choices. As I've said before: to each, his own dinner. In fact, I view such choices as akin to religious ones; we can take in information, we can listen to opinions, we can research, but at a certain point we decide

on our own direction. And our cultural ties to food run deep—something that can get lost when writings about veganism and vegetarianism turn reductive (Exhibit A: Alicia Silverstone, who in her book *The Kind Diet* dismisses a food that has been consumed by human beings for thousands of years with one simplistic phrase: "Eggs are weird").

In fact, I'm reluctant to even use the word "vegetarian," as you might have noticed from the title and subtitle of this book. Why? Well, I've long thought that in a focus on vegetarianism, what tends to get short shrift are the actual vegetables, perhaps because the dishes are defined by what's not in them rather than by what is. What I mean is that I want to tell you to cook, say, Carrot and Ginger Soup with Quick-Pickled Beet (page 64) not because it doesn't include bacon (because what does bacon have to do with anything?). I want you to cook it because it's easy and it tastes great. It's why I wish we could come up with another term for Meatless Mondays. As Steven Shapin wrote in the *New Yorker* in 2007, "Vegetarianism has always been less about why you should eat plants than about why you shouldn't eat animals." I'm hoping that changes, and I want to be part of that change. So, I would rather think about this as a vegetable cookbook, not a vegetarian one. It's about what's on the plate rather than what's missing.

Whatever term you use, the challenges for single cooks remain: How do you shop efficiently without buying excess food that goes bad in your fridge's "rotter"? How do you satisfy what I call "hanger" (hunger meets anger) at the end of a long workday without resorting to takeout? How do you cook in a way that makes productive use of what you buy without resulting in a mountain of tedious leftovers? I hope to continue to answer those questions, in a vegetable context. But I want to do more.

I said I resist most zealotry, but there is one thing I've felt compelled to proselytize about, and that's the importance of cooking. Particularly, it's been my ongoing mission to get single folks—31 million of us in the United States alone—to realize that cooking for ourselves, despite the obstacles, is a worthwhile, satisfying, potentially meditative, possibly invigorating, and maybe even delightful endeavor. If you truly want to take care of yourself, if you want to know just what's going into your body, you've got to learn to DIY dinner. Since vegetables can be more challenging to cook than meat—we're less familiar with them, and they require a little more care to bring out all their best qualities—the bar is raised for single vegetarians. At the same time, even if they don't live alone, vegetarians might be even more interested in single-serving recipes than others because they might be the only vegetarian in the house.

Ultimately, I hope that readers find as much inspiration in vegetables as I have, and bring that inspiration to their own table, whether it's set for vegetarians or onivores, for one or a crowd.

# Acknowledgments

THOMAS MANN ONCE WROTE, "A writer is somebody for whom writing is more difficult than it is for other people." If that doesn't make sense to you, then you haven't ever tried to put words to paper or screen. For those of us who have, we appreciate all the help we can get in the struggle. Many, many people helped me write this book in ways large and small, in many cases without even knowing it. I'm going to try to account here for as much as I can of the help I've received; please forgive any omissions.

Thank you to:

My sister, Rebekah, and brother-in-law Peter, who graciously allowed me to crash on their Maine homestead for a year while I worked, and didn't object when my need to write overtook my promises to help with chores. And to our sister Teri for visiting and cooking her heart out when she did.

Marcus Brauchli, Raju Narisetti, Liz Spayd, Kevin Sullivan, and other PTB (powers that be) at the *Washington Post*, for allowing me the year off, and my colleagues in the Food and Travel sections—Bonnie Benwick, Zofia Smardz, Tim Carman, Andrea Sachs, Becky Krystal, Jane Touzalin, and Jim Webster—for holding down the fort so ably in my absence.

Aaron Wehner and the rest of the stellar team at Ten Speed Press, especially my editor, Jenny Wapner. I challenged her to pull none of her punches and to push me to make every recipe, essay—indeed, paragraph, sentence, and word—more effective, and she did. Copy editor Clancy Drake efficiently and cheerfully buffed out all the remaining rough spots. Also to Kristin Casemore for her vigorous and responsive promotion work, and to designer Toni Tajima for translating the ideas so beautifully onto the page. I couldn't be more thrilled to have worked with the hilarious and talented photographer Matt Armendariz, who with stylist Adam Pearson gave my dishes the clean, modern, warm look I love so much. I'm a big fan.

The best agents an author could hope for: Lisa Ekus and Sally Ekus, who do so much more than just negotiate contracts, acting as partners throughout the process.

Every farmer of the many who have grown a beautiful vegetable or fruit that has made it into my kitchen, onto my plate, and then into my body, including those at Tree and Leaf, Moondance, Two Toad, Chick, Kuhn, Next Step, Toigo, Endless Summer Harvest, and many more. And to Robin Shuster, Ann Yonkers, Bernie Price, and all the other founders, managers, volunteers, and other vendors at my favorite farmers' markets at home and on my travels, including Dupont FreshFarm, 14th and U, North Berwick,

Ferry Building, Hollywood, Union Square, both Portlands, and more.

All the chefs who do right by vegetables for inspiring me with their dishes, including Amanda Cohen, Rich Landau, Kate Jacoby, Daniel Patterson, David Kinch, Thomas McNaughton, Dan Barber, Frank Ruta, José Andrés, Cedric Maupillier, Ashley Christensen, Mike Lata, Sean Brock, and more.

Independent bookstore owners for fighting the good fight, including Don and Sam Lindgren at Rabelais Books, Celia Sack at Omnivore Books, Kelly Justice at Fountain Books, and Daniel Goldin at Boswell Books. And to fellow cookbook authors, food-world friends, and writers for moral support, including Andrea Nguyen, Sally Swift, Patricia Jinich, David Lebovitz, Jane Black, Virginia Willis, Nathalie Dupree, Penny de los Santos, Sarah-Kate Gillingham-Ryan, Kathy Gunst, Dorie Greenspan, and Kim O'Donnel.

*Washington Post* readers who have emailed with questions, comments, praise, and criticism for my columns and recipes, helping keep me on my toes.

Christopher Bellonci and Edouard Fontenot for allowing me to hole up in their beautiful house in Boston while they were away, for the final push to finish the book.

The dozens of people who helped immeasurably by testing recipes, making them for themselves and sometimes for friends and family and giving me feedback on everything from the hunt for ingredients to the process to the all-important result. The recipes are far better thanks to their help: Bonnie Deahl, Tara Bellucci, Judy Landry, Gavin Hilgemeier, Christine Smith, Nisha Patel, Ann Cochran, Victoria Solomon, Judy Shertzer, Emily Kehe, Kristina Allison, Joshua Bloom, Carol Blymire, Carol Penn-Romine, Arnessa M. Garrett, Rina Rapuano, Necee Regis, Jill Trudeau Marquard, Jessica Wonderlich, Erin Meister, Amy Rogers, Rebekah Denn, Rashda Khan, Jessica Erfer, Jennifer Kildee, Jamie Haines, Gary Bowden and Mark Ziomek, Corrin Phillips, Barbara McGrath, Rebecca Vitale, Kim Watson, Ashley Lusk, Amelia Nuss, Alison McQuade, Rachel Alabiso, Lynne Viera, Christy Goldfinch and Frank Whetstine, Christopher Bellonci and Edouard Fontenot, Annabelle Blake, Stefanie Gans, Nycci Nellis, Melissa Hamilton, Mallory deGolian, Lisa Amore, Linda Haas, Lilly Jan, Laura Trevino, Katie Hards, Karen Barone, and JoAnn Erfer.

And, finally, Carl J. "Spanky" Mason for giving me the excuse to cook for two now and again, for dealing with my yearlong absence—and for welcoming me back.

# How to Use This Book

ECIPES ARE GUIDELINES, and I want you to treat mine that way.

For instance, in "Forget the Clock, Remember Your Food" (page 34), I resist specifying timing, especially in the parts of the recipe that go particularly quickly and variably. But I also want readers to use their own judgment about quantity and ingredients, something that should be easier for single cooks to do than others, because there is nobody else to please. When you start to cook, ask yourself: How hungry am I? What do I feel like eating? What am I in the mood for? That means that even after you pick out a recipe that looks good, decide whether you want it spicier or not, fattier or not, bigger or smaller. I don't mean to cede responsibility here; obviously, I developed these recipes to create a result that I find delicious, but feel free to use them as a jumping-off point and to make them your own.

That might include adjusting the quantity, or even adding more dishes if you're composing dinner for multiple people. As the subtitle promises, the vast majority of dishes in the book serve one, but as I learned when promoting *Serve Yourself*, two-person households also need smaller-scale recipes. The most obvious way to adapt these recipes for couples is to merely double the ingredients, but another way is to treat these dishes as part of a larger meal, keeping their size intact but adding side dishes, salads, bread—or even other courses. For example, in the case of pasta or soup recipes, couples can easily share the dish as a first course.

In Chapter 7 I include recipes for staples to keep on hand for use in other dishes. This is a smart strategy for single cooks who want to maximize their time by making larger-quantity recipes without forcing themselves to eat the same thing day in and day out. Obviously, couples and larger groups can feel free to use the entire quantity at once rather than refrigerating or freezing the leftovers. Or, if they still want the advantage of those building-block ingredients, they can multiply the recipe.

That brings me to scaling. In most cases scaling up is pretty straightforward, but watch out for the spices, which usually don't need to be doubled, or tripled because their strength tends to multiply exponentially. This is especially true of the more pungent spices: crushed red pepper flakes and other chiles, cumin, peppercorns, curry, cardamom, anise, smoked paprika, cloves, and the like. But really, it's best to taste as you go when trying to multiply any freshly ground spice. By the same token, when you're cutting a large-quantity recipe down to single-serving size, something singles are accustomed to doing when using conventional cookbooks, you often need to err on the side of a little more spice than you might have thought.

These recipes are mostly vegetarian, with the exception of the very occasional use of anchovies, fish sauce, and the like, but those ingredients are optional. I'm not vegan, so dairy and eggs are included where I see fit, as is honey, but vegans should be able to see fairly obvious ways to adapt these recipes, either by merely leaving something out or by substituting a vegan equivalent such as soy milk or nondairy cheese. I have not tested the recipes with those substitutions, so I'm trusting readers to make their own decisions, based on their own experience with those products. I also hope no vegetarian readers will be offended by my suggestions for ways carnivores can add meat and seafood to recipes if desired. This reflects my eat-and-let-eat philosophy.

One important step on the road to making satisfying food for yourself (and anyone else) is to learn your preferred seasoning, and by seasoning I mean salting. I encourage readers to salt their food to their own taste, and the best way to do that is to add salt as you're cooking, which means you need to get into the habit of tasting your food as you go along. If you don't think that salt makes a difference in your food, try this exercise:

- Make a soup recipe in this book (say, Carrot and Ginger Soup with Quick-Pickled Beet) with two important changes: don't add any salt at all, and before you add the garnish, divide the soup into two halves, and keep each warm.
- Put 1 teaspoon of kosher or coarse sea salt into a little glass dish; those are my preferred

salts, for taste and because they're easy to grab with your fingers.
- Add salt to half of the soup a pinch at a time, tasting as you go, and pay attention to how the flavors start to develop.
- Keep adding until you get to the point where you think that the soup tastes too salty—that is, you taste more salt than you do carrots and ginger.
- Now look to see how much salt is left; measure it if you like, and subtract that from 1 teaspoon.
- Try the exercise again with the second half of the soup, this time with the goal of stopping just short of that too-salty flavor. Make the measurement calculation again, if you like, and take note: That is about how much salt you like in a recipe of this size, and that proportion is what you should be going for when you're cooking. If you'd rather not measure, that's fine too; it's better to get to the point where salting becomes intuitive. You'll be a better cook.

By the way, if you're worried that all this will cause you to increase your sodium intake, remember that you'll get far less sodium from home-cooked meals than any processed foods, so you're a step ahead. (The research is muddy on the connection between sodium and high blood pressure, anyway, but that's another story.)

Since I don't cook meat, I love using nuts and seeds of all kinds to add crunchy texture and a little protein to my dishes, but when you're in a hurry it might seem annoying to be toasting just a tablespoon or two of, say, pumpkin seeds to top off a single-serving dish. Do what I do and get in the habit of toasting a cup or two at a time.

They're great to snack on (especially if you have self-control, which I don't), they keep for a week or two in an airtight container at room temperature, and doing this will save you one more step when you're cooking. After burning too many trays of nuts because I took my eye (and mind) off them, I prefer the stovetop method of toasting. But if your oven is already preheated, you can slide a pan of nuts in; just make sure to check every few minutes, react quickly once that beautiful toasty aroma fills the air, and quickly transfer them to a cool plate or pan so they stop cooking. If you're feeling lazy, you can buy already roasted nuts at the store; just be aware that they will go stale sooner than unroasted ones, so it's best to store them in the freezer.

That philosophy can extend to other ingredients, too. When your oven is already hot, take the opportunity to roast more vegetables than called for in a specific recipe. You'll be glad to find them in the refrigerator the next day, just waiting to be chopped up for a quick salad, pureed into a soup, or eaten on a little bread as a snack.

Whether it's nuts, spices, herbs, or produce, one of the problems that can vex single cooks more than any other is this: Why buy large quantities of ingredients when you only need a little bit? That's why I strive in this book to help you use up ingredients in multiple recipes. However, you are the best judge of your pantry, refrigerator, and freezer space, so while I include a particular spice in a recipe because I think it's worth seeking out and want you to try it, I also won't be offended if you need to make a substitution or omission.

If you've got room on your counter or in a drawer for a mortar and pestle, or a repurposed coffee grinder you can dedicate to spices, I urge you to buy spices whole, not already ground. Spices (like coffee) last so much longer if left whole and then ground right before you use them. Since it takes single folks that much longer to go through spices, this is no small matter. And if you're wondering if a spice is past its prime, just remember: The nose knows.

# Storing and Using Up Extra Ingredients

Here's my cheat sheet for finding ways to use up ingredients you have left over from making one or more of the recipes in this book.

## Fresh Herbs

Home-grown and farmers' market herbs last longer than store-bought. If you have space to grow them on a windowsill or patio, or, best of all, in a garden, you can pick at will—this is the best option of all. The second-best option is herbs from farmers' markets (and, increasingly, grocery stores) that include the roots; just stick those in water and put them on your countertop, where they'll stay fresh for days. Sturdy herbs such as basil, mint, and parsley are best treated like cut flowers: strip off the bottom leaves so they won't be immersed, then cut the stems on the diagonal and put them in a glass of fresh water on the countertop or in the fridge (preferably in plain sight), changing the water and cutting the stems every day or two. Store more delicate herbs, such as cilantro, oregano, thyme, and dill, by wrapping them in a damp paper towel, enclosing in a perforated plastic bag (I like to use newspaper delivery bags), and refrigerating for up to 1 week.

**Use leftover fresh basil in:**

Baby Eggplant Parm (page 74)

Basil Goddess Dressing (page 31)

Bean and Israeli Couscous Soup (page 66)

Creamy Green Gazpacho (page 61)

Fusilli with Corn Sauce (page 100)

Indonesian Tofu and Egg Wraps (page 55)

Spicy Basil Tofu Fried Rice (page 106)

Strawberry-Basil Shortcake in a Jar (page 131)

Summer Succotash (page 178)

Thai-Style Kabocha Squash and Tofu Curry (page 117)

**Use leftover fresh mint in:**

Asian Bean and Barley Salad (page 16)

Asparagus with Romesco Blanco (page 76)

Blueberry Ginger Smoothie (page 136)

Lime Ginger Vinaigrette (page 23)

Minty Pea Soup with Pea and Feta Toast (page 56)

Plum-Pomegranate Smoothie (page 137)

Pomegranate-Glazed Eggplant (page 91)

Spring Pea and Lettuce Tart (page 80)

**Use leftover fresh cilantro in:**

Asian Bean and Barley Salad (page 16)

Cool, Spicy Mango Yogurt Soup (page 57)

Lime Ginger Vinaigrette (page 23)

continued >

< Use leftover fresh cilantro in, continued

Potato and Bean Tostadas with Avocado–Green Onion Salsa (page 113)

Roasted Cauliflower and Green Beans with Chipotle Sauce (page 81)

Smoky Cabbage and Noodles with Glazed Tempeh (page 27)

Spinach Enchiladas (page 85)

Use leftover fresh parsley in:

Lime Ginger Vinaigrette (page 23)

Tomato-Braised Green Beans and New Potatoes (page 118)

## Half an Avocado

Store by rubbing the exposed flesh with olive oil, then wrapping tightly in plastic wrap (press the wrap directly against the flesh of the avocado) and refrigerating for 3 to 4 days. Cut off any browned spots before using.

Use in:

Creamy Green Gazpacho (page 61)

Enfrijoladas with Egg, Avocado, and Onion (page 110)

Guaca-Chi (page 148; half-batch)

Potato and Bean Tostadas with Avocado–Green Onion Salsa (page 113)

Tomato-Kale-Avocado Smoothie (page 137)

## Half a Lemon or Lime

Store by wrapping tightly in plastic wrap and refrigerating for 4 to 5 days. Or juice it and freeze the juice in ice cube trays, transfer the cubes to ziplock bags, and store in the freezer for up to 6 months.

Use lime in:

Basil Goddess Dressing (page 31)

Bean and Poblano Soup with Cinnamon Croutons (page 63)

Cool, Spicy Mango Yogurt Soup (page 57)

Grilled Pecan Butter and Peach Spread Sandwich (page 47)

Guaca-Chi (page 148)

Kale and Caramelized Onion Quesadilla (page 54)

Lime Ginger Vinaigrette (page 23)

Poblano Tapenade (page 151)

Potato and Bean Tostadas with Avocado–Green Onion Salsa (page 113)

Roasted Sweet Potato with Southeast Asian Topping (page 87)

Roasted Sweet Potato with Southwestern Topping (page 87)

Tomato-Kale-Avocado Smoothie (page 137)

Use lemon in:

Apple-Walnut Smoothie (page 137)

Faux Tart with Instant Lemon Ginger Custard (page 128)

Grilled Pistachio Butter and Cherry Spread Sandwich (page 47)

Lemon Chile Vinaigrette (page 26)

Ricotta, Zucchini, and Radicchio Sandwich (page 52)

Spaghetti with Root-to-Leaf Radish (page 103)

Spicy Kale Salad with Miso-Mushroom Omelet (page 24)

## Half a Jalapeño

Store by drying it off thoroughly, wrapping it in plastic wrap, and refrigerating for 3 to 4 days.

Use in:

Cool, Spicy Mango Yogurt Soup (page 57)

Creamy Green Gazpacho (page 61)

Potato and Bean Tostadas with Avocado–Green Onion Salsa (page 113)

Spinach Enchiladas (page 85)

Tofu, Grilled Cabbage, and Poblano Tapenade Sandwich (page 49)

## Celery Stalks (from a Bunch)

Store by wrapping the remaining bunch in aluminum foil—really—and refrigerating for up to 2 weeks. If you need to recrisp celery, cut off one end and stick it in a glass of water for half an hour.

Use in:

Celery Soup with Apple and Blue Cheese (page 62)

Creamy Green Gazpacho (page 61)

Green Gumbo (page 58)

## Part of a Can of Beans

Store by draining, rinsing, and transferring to an airtight plastic or glass container. Drizzle with a little olive oil and refrigerate for up to 1 week. To freeze, skip the olive oil step, but cover with water and freeze for several months. (If storing homemade beans, refrigerate or freeze in their cooking liquid.)

Use in:

Asian Bean and Barley Salad (page 16)

Bean and Israeli Couscous Soup (page 66)

Bean and Poblano Soup with Cinnamon Croutons (page 63)

Curried Mushroom Bean Burgers (page 42)

Enfrijoladas with Egg, Avocado, and Onion (page 110)

Grilled Greens, Chickpea, and Peppadew Sandwich (page 50)

Potato and Bean Tostadas with Avocado–Green Onion Salsa (page 113)

Roasted Sweet Potato with Southwestern Topping (page 87)

## Chapter 1

# SALADS and DRESSINGS

When you grow your own vegetables, late spring through early fall are the salad days, literally: you can step into the garden as soon as you're hungry, snip this green and that into a basket, pick a few ripe tomatoes, peppers, and cukes, pull up a carrot or two, grab some herbs, and come back into your kitchen with the makings of an easy, quick dinner. That's what my sister and I did during much of the peak growing season of the year I spent in Maine helping her and her husband work the land. When the produce is within-minutes fresh, sometimes it seems a shame to do much more than chop it up raw and dress it simply.

That's the fantasy. Once I was back in Washington, though, I had to contend to reality. I work long hours and depend on produce from farmers' markets and a nearby Whole Foods rather than on anything I grow myself. But I still love to make salads, which can be the single cook's best friend—if you only learn to treat your fridge like a salad bar, with lots of ingredients prepped and some of them precooked.

Here's how I like to think about salads generally, and not just in spring or summer: start with the right seasonal vegetables, left raw or cooked gently; toss them with a grain in the form of rice or noodles (or slice up some bread to eat on the side); get a little protein from legumes, nuts, cheese, an egg, and/or tofu; and spark things up with the right pickles, dressings, or other condiments. All these components are within your reach when they're ready-made or quick to make. Get in the habit of stocking your fridge, and you'll rarely visit a salad bar—other than your own—again.

*If you're ready for this salad, there's no stove required, keeping you as cool as the cucumbers in it. And by ready, I mean that you've listened to my pleas to cook things like a pot of beans when you have time on the weekend, and that you're storing these basics for a use like this one. I give directions for cooking the barley from scratch here, but as with the beans, it's a better strategy to already have it around. (If you do, use ³/₄ cup cooked and cooled barley; see Note.) This dish was shamelessly adapted from a recipe in the fabulous Bean by Bean by eminent vegetarian author Crescent Dragonwagon. You can, of course, mess with it further, using whatever seasonal vegetables strike your fancy. My favorite beans to use here are chickpeas, but others work well, too. For the barley, you can substitute brown rice (page 177), farro, or another grain.*

# ASIAN BEAN and BARLEY SALAD

Combine the barley and water in a small saucepan over medium-high heat. Bring to a boil, reduce the heat, cover, and cook until the barley is tender and has absorbed almost all of the liquid, 50 to 60 minutes. Remove from the heat and let it rest, covered, for 10 minutes before fluffing with a fork and letting it cool to room temperature.

Sprinkle the peanuts into a small skillet over medium-high heat. Cook, shaking the pan frequently, until the peanuts have darkened and become fragrant, just a few minutes. Immediately transfer them to a plate to cool; if you leave them to cool in the pan, they can burn. Once they are cool, chop them.

Toss together the barley, beans, peas, sugar snap peas, carrot, green onion, cucumber, cilantro or mint, and ginger in a medium bowl. Drizzle the oil and vinegar over the mixture and toss to combine; taste and add salt if needed. Transfer to a serving bowl, top with the peanuts, and eat.

NOTE: If you want to make more barley than you need for this recipe, keep the 3-to-1 water-to-barley ratio and, after cooling, freeze extra servings of barley in airtight ziplock bags (see "A Vacuum Shortcut," page 171) for up to 6 months.

³/₄ cup water

¹/₄ cup pearled barley

2 tablespoons unsalted raw peanuts

¹/₂ cup cooked and lightly drained beans, preferably homemade (page 175), or low-sodium canned, thoroughly rinsed and drained

¹/₄ cup fresh or thawed frozen peas

¹/₄ cup sugar snap peas, thinly sliced

1 small carrot, scrubbed and halved lengthwise, then cut into thin half-moons

1 green onion, trimmed and thinly sliced

¹/₂ small cucumber, peeled and cut into ¹/₂-inch chunks

¹/₄ cup cilantro or mint leaves, chopped

1 tablespoon grated fresh ginger (from a 2-inch piece of peeled ginger root)

2 teaspoons toasted sesame oil

1 tablespoon rice vinegar, preferably unseasoned

Sea salt

*I can't live without poached eggs, especially after adopting food scientist Harold McGee's tip: strain out the thinnest, most watery part of the egg white before you slip the egg into simmering water. It prevents the formation of those wispy strands that make the egg so stringy and unsightly. This technique works best if you use a perforated spoon (like the one food writer Michael Ruhlman sells on Open Sky), if you don't have that, you can use a coarse-mesh strainer, but it takes longer.*

# PERFECT POACHED EGG

Bring several inches of heavily salted water to a boil in a large sauté pan. Decrease the heat slightly so that the water is bubbling gently but not boiling.

**Kosher salt**

**1  egg**

Crack the egg into a small dish or ramekin, then pour it into a deep perforated spoon held over a dish. Swirl the egg around in the spoon so that the thinnest of the white dribbles through the holes and into the dish. (Alternatively, you can crack the egg into a coarse-mesh strainer set over a cup, and let it sit for several minutes, undisturbed, while the thin white drains into the cup.)

Pour out the thin white from the dish or cup and discard, then tip the egg from the spoon or the strainer into a cup. Then gently tip it into the bubbling water. Cook the egg until the white is set but the yolk still wobbles when you press it, 3 to 4 minutes. Use the perforated spoon or strainer to transfer the egg to a plate lined with a paper towel. If you want to keep the egg warm for up to 20 minutes or so, transfer it instead to a bowl of very warm (120°F) water, then to the paper towel–lined plate to drain.

*My ramen experience started, as is the case with so many Americans, when I was a college student desperate to make my dollar stretch by using it to buy a twelve-pack of instant ramen with the salty little seasoning packets. Thankfully, a trip to Japan—including the Shin-Yokahama Raumen Museum, which is more like a ramen amusement park than a museum—expanded my horizons. I was so busy eating bowl after bowl of ramen that I completely missed out on abura soba, broth-free noodles dressed in chile oil and topped with various vegetables plus the requisite runny-yolk egg. Instead, I discovered it at Pai men Miyake in Portland, Maine, but I dream of returning to Tokyo for more immersion. In the meantime, I make my own take on it at home, using the noodles from a packet of instant ramen and throwing away the seasoning packet. One thing's for sure: it beats the heck out of what I ate during my poor-college-student days. Despite my reverence for ramen, by the way, you can make this with other noodles, such as soba, udon, or even soaked rice noodles.*

# COLD SPICY RAMEN NOODLES with TOFU and KIMCHI

Sprinkle the peanuts into a small skillet over medium-high heat. Cook, shaking the pan frequently, until the peanuts have darkened and become fragrant, just a few minutes. Immediately transfer them to a plate to cool; if you leave them to cool in the pan, they can burn. Once they are cool, chop them.

Cook the ramen in a saucepan of boiling water for 3 minutes, then drain and plop into a serving bowl. Drizzle with the chile oil and sprinkle with the garlic while tossing the noodles. Let the noodles cool to room temperature, or chill in the refrigerator.

Top with the kimchi, carrot, green onion, tofu, egg, and peanuts, drizzle with Sriracha, and eat.

2 tablespoons unsalted, raw peanuts

2 ounces ramen noodles (from one package instant ramen)

1 tablespoon chile oil, homemade (page 168) or store-bought

1 clove garlic, finely chopped

1/4 cup Cabbage Kimchi, homemade (page 163) or store-bought, chopped, with its liquid

1 small carrot, scrubbed and finely shredded

1 green onion, trimmed and thinly sliced

1/2 cup Marinated and Baked Tofu (page 170) or store-bought baked or extra-firm tofu

1 Perfect Poached Egg (page 17)

Sriracha (optional)

*I love Israeli couscous, sometimes called pearl couscous, for its texture; it has much more bite than the smaller, fluffy couscous. That makes it the perfect starchy base for warm salads in which other ingredients offer a little crunch, too—in this case, quickly broiled broccoli, raw carrot pieces, and crunchy cashews. Even though you use just a little of them in this recipe, fight the urge to skip the Quick-Pickled Golden Raisins (page 172); they pull everything together with a little spicy punch.*

# CURRIED BROCCOLI and WARM ISRAELI COUSCOUS SALAD

Turn the oven broiler on, with a rack in the closest position to the flame or element.

Cut the florets off the broccoli head. Peel the stem, and cut the stem and the florets into 1/2-inch pieces. Drizzle them with 1 teaspoon of the olive oil, sprinkle with the curry powder and a little salt, and broil until they are lightly browned, watching carefully so they don't burn.

Pour the remaining 2 teaspoons of olive oil into a small saucepan; place the pan over medium heat. When the oil shimmers, add the garlic, tomatoes, and carrot, and cook, stirring occasionally, until the tomatoes collapse. Stir in the couscous, water, and a generous sprinkling of salt. Reduce the heat to medium-low, cover, and cook, stirring occasionally, until the couscous has swelled, absorbed the water, and become just tender, 10 to 12 minutes. Remove the pan from the heat.

While the couscous is cooking, sprinkle the cashews into a small skillet over medium-high heat. Cook, shaking the pan frequently, until the cashews have darkened and become fragrant, just a few minutes. Immediately transfer them to a plate to cool; if you leave them to cool in the pan, they can burn. Once they are cool, chop them.

Let the couscous rest for a few minutes, then stir in the arugula and raisins. Transfer to a bowl, top with the broiled broccoli and cashews, and eat.

1 **very small head broccoli (4 or 5 florets), or several stalks broccolini**

1 **tablespoon extra-virgin olive oil**

1 **teaspoon Madras curry powder**

 **Sea salt**

1 **clove garlic, chopped**

4 **large cherry tomatoes, quartered**

1 **small carrot, scrubbed and cut into 1/2-inch slices**

1/3 **cup Israeli couscous**

1/3 **cup water**

2 **tablespoons unsalted, raw cashews**

1 **cup lightly packed arugula leaves, chopped**

1 **tablespoon Quick-Pickled Golden Raisins (page 172)**

*Now that I've learned how silky kale becomes when you massage it, I include it in all sorts of salads. A farmer I met in Maine told me she likes the combination of kale and mango, and sure enough, so do I, especially in a preparation that evokes the classic French Niçoise salad—well, except for the lack of tuna, the absence of green beans, the disappearance of olives... Okay, it's really far from a Niçoise, I guess, but with the potato and egg, it's got a little je ne sais quoi, don't you think?*

# KALE and MANGO NIÇOISE SALAD

Bring a medium saucepan of salted water to a simmer, and add the potato. Simmer until barely tender, 6 to 8 minutes, then drain the pieces.

Toss the kale in a serving bowl with half the vinaigrette and a light sprinkling of salt. Top with the potato, egg, mango, and radish, drizzle with the remaining vinaigrette, and eat.

1 small waxy potato, peeled and cut into 1-inch cubes

2 cups (about 4 ounces) lacinato or other kale leaves, thinly sliced and massaged (see below)

2 to 3 tablespoons Lime Ginger Vinaigrette (page 23)

Sea salt

1 Perfectly Creamy Hard-Cooked Egg (page 167), peeled and cut into eighths

Flesh from ¹/₂ small mango, such as Champagne or Ataulfo variety, cubed

2 small radishes, trimmed and thinly sliced

## Massaging Kale

Kale does what we all do when subjected to a good massage: it melts. Well, it doesn't melt completely, but it does turn silky and vivid green as the cells break down.

Why on earth would you massage kale? Because it makes it more pleasant to eat raw. And it's very easy. I had read different takes on the idea, all of them using some combination of olive oil, lemon juice, and salt, and that works, but I found it got the kale more broken down than I wanted, almost to the point where it seemed cooked, and too wet. So I do it with just two ingredients: kale and my bare hands. Couldn't be simpler, and it's therapeutic, too (for you and the kale). (continued opposite)

Strip the kale leaves from the stems, and reserve the stems for another use. Thinly slice the kale leaves. (One easy way to do this is to chiffonade them: stack a bunch of them, roll them tightly into a cigar shape, and thinly slice from one end.) Add them to a mixing bowl as you work. Then pick them up by the handfuls and vigorously squeeze, repeating until you have worked your way through the kale, as if you're kneading bread. Keep picking up and squeezing until the kale has deepened in color and turned a silky texture but is still fluffy. It should take just a few minutes.

Use it however you like, simply dressed in a vinaigrette with the seasonal vegetables of your choice, or in such dishes as Kale and Mango Niçoise Salad (page 22) or Indonesian Tofu and Egg Wraps (page 55).

*I learned in culinary school, as did so many others, that the classic proportions for a vinaigrette are three parts oil to one part vinegar (or other acidic component). Well, I like things lighter and tarter than that, so I go halfsies instead. This easy dressing follows that principle, and adds a little honey to compensate for all that lime. Use it when you want something particularly bright: on greens, bean and grain salads, tomatoes, and avocados, or, for seafood eaters, as a marinade for grilled fish or shrimp. Store it in an airtight container in the refrigerator for up to 1 week.*

# LIME GINGER VINAIGRETTE

**MAKES ABOUT 1 CUP**

Combine the lime juice, oil, ginger, honey, and chopped herbs in a small jar fitted with a lid, close the lid tightly, and vigorously shake to emulsify the dressing. Taste and add salt as needed plus more honey if desired, and shake again.

1/2 **cup freshly squeezed lime juice (from 4 to 6 limes)**

1/2 **cup sunflower or other neutral vegetable oil**

1 **tablespoon finely grated ginger (from a 2-inch piece of peeled ginger)**

1 **tablespoon honey, plus more as needed**

1 **tablespoon chopped parsley, mint, or cilantro leaves**

**Sea salt**

*When I ate at Animal in Los Angeles, the last thing I expected was to be wowed by a vegetarian dish, but sure enough, a baby kale salad doused in lemon and chile oil and tossed with Pecorino and pumpernickel crumbs was a standout on an otherwise carnivorous menu. When I brought the idea home, I subbed pecans for the breadcrumbs and added a mushroom omelet to turn it into a single-serving meal. It's quick to make, light, and yet satisfying (especially with a hunk of bread). If you don't have Lemon Chile Vinaigrette (page 26) on hand, make some! Or you can substitute freshly squeezed lemon juice, chile oil, and a little salt.*

# SPICY KALE SALAD with MISO-MUSHROOM OMELET

Sprinkle the pecans into a small skillet over medium-high heat. Cook, shaking the pan frequently, until the nuts start to brown and become fragrant, a few minutes. Immediately transfer them to a plate to cool; if you leave them to cool in the pan, they can burn. Once they are cool, chop them.

Whisk together the miso and water in a small bowl, then whisk in the egg until well combined.

Heat the olive oil in a small, preferably nonstick, skillet over medium-high heat. Once the oil shimmers, add the mushrooms and cook, stirring occasionally, until they collapse. Spoon the mushrooms onto a plate, leaving as much oil in the pan as you can.

Return the skillet to the heat and reduce the heat to medium. Add a little more oil if the pan seems dry. Pour in the miso-egg mixture; cook briefly, just until it sets on the bottom; lift the edges of the set egg on one side and tilt the pan toward that side so the uncooked egg runs underneath, and do this a time or two more until the egg isn't runny on top. Spoon the mushrooms down the middle and fold the eggs over the mushrooms to form an omelet. Cook briefly on each side, until the omelet is just cooked through. Transfer it to a cutting board to cool.

Toss the massaged kale with the vinaigrette in a serving bowl. Once the omelet has cooled, chop it into bite-sized pieces. Add the omelet pieces and Pecorino to the kale and toss to combine, then grind a generous amount of pepper on top. Sprinkle on the pecans, and eat.

1 tablespoon unsalted raw pecan halves

1 teaspoon white miso

1 teaspoon water

1 egg

1 tablespoon extra-virgin olive oil, plus more if needed

1 cup chopped cremini, oyster, hen of the woods, or other meaty mushrooms

2 cups lacinato or other kale leaves, stripped from their stems, thinly sliced and massaged (see page 22)

2 tablespoons Lemon Chile Vinaigrette (page 26)

1 ounce coarsely grated Pecorino Romano cheese

Freshly ground black pepper

*The tang of lemon and the tickle of heat—what could be better when you want to brighten up a salad? I love this on raw kale, whose slight bitterness cries out for something pungent. Try it on Spicy Kale Salad with Miso-Mushroom Omelet (page 24). It's great drizzled on hearty roasted root vegetables such as potatoes, sweet potatoes, carrots, parsnips, beets, and the like. And it makes a lively marinade for grilled tofu, chicken, and seafood.*

# LEMON CHILE VINAIGRETTE

## MAKES ABOUT 1 CUP

Smash the garlic with the side of a chef's knife, sprinkle with the salt, and finely chop the two together. Smear it with the side of the knife to create a paste, and transfer it to a small glass jar.

Add the lemon juice, chile oil, olive oil, mustard, honey, and several grinds of black pepper. Screw on the jar's lid and shake to combine. Taste and add more salt as needed. Refrigerate for up to 2 weeks.

1 clove garlic

$1/2$ teaspoon kosher salt, plus more to taste

$1/3$ cup freshly squeezed lemon juice (from 2 to 3 large lemons)

$1/4$ cup Chile Oil, homemade (page 168) or store-bought

$1/4$ cup extra-virgin olive oil

2 teaspoons Dijon mustard

2 teaspoons honey

Freshly ground black pepper

*Here's a slaw turned into a main course: the cabbage keeps its crunch and gains flavor from the grill, while udon noodles add their silky goodness and tempeh offers a touch of protein. It's the antithesis of the watery summer slaw. If you'd rather have it as a side dish, leave out the tempeh. If you've popped a whole cabbage on the grill, you've got the makings of a dish for a couple, or a crowd, instead of one: just multiply at will. Omnivores, feel free to sub in grilled chicken, shrimp, or cubes of pork.*

# SMOKY CABBAGE and NOODLES with GLAZED TEMPEH

Cook the udon noodles according to the package directions, drain, and toss in a medium bowl with the sesame oil.

While the udon is cooking, sprinkle the peanuts into a small skillet over medium-high heat. Cook, shaking the pan frequently, until the peanuts have darkened and become fragrant, just a few minutes. Immediately transfer them to a plate to cool; if you leave them to cool in the pan, they can burn. Once they are cool, chop them.

Pour the vegetable oil into a medium skillet over medium-high heat; when the oil starts to shimmer, add the tempeh slices and cook until golden brown, about 3 minutes per side. Turn off the heat, pour in the soy sauce, and toss to glaze the tempeh. Transfer to a plate to cool, and chop into bite-size pieces.

Add the grilled cabbage, salad greens, green onion, and carrot to the udon noodles, sprinkle the vinegar over, and toss to combine. Taste and add soy sauce if desired. Transfer to a serving bowl, sprinkle with the cilantro leaves and peanuts, and eat.

2 ounces dried udon noodles

1 teaspoon toasted sesame oil

2 tablespoons unsalted, raw peanuts

2 teaspoons vegetable oil

3 ounces tempeh, cut into 1/4-inch slices

1 1/2 teaspoons low-sodium soy sauce, plus more to taste

1 cup Grilled Cabbage (page 165)

1/4 cup mixed salad greens, chopped

1 green onion, trimmed and thinly sliced

1 small carrot, scrubbed and shaved into strips with a vegetable peeler

2 teaspoons rice vinegar, preferably unseasoned

1 tablespoon chopped cilantro leaves

*I thought I was being so clever when I came in from the garden with tomatoes and beets, spied some farmers' market peaches on the countertop and thought: three round things, two of them fruits and one of them an earthy root vegetable, all in season at the same time. Wouldn't they go well together? Of course, nothing is new, as I learned when I looked on my bookshelf and found a beautifully simple salad with that same triumvirate in Roy Finamore's lovely book Tasty. His version is delicious, but I can't leave well enough alone, so I like to stack a smallish version of each of the three, sprinkle them with feta, and drizzle with Walnut Oregano Vinaigrette (page 30). (If you don't have the vinaigrette on hand and don't want to make it, you can substitute drizzles of extra-virgin olive oil, red wine vinegar, crumbled walnuts, and a little salt.) Feel free to substitute your favorite lettuce for the base if your beets don't have their lovely veined greens attached. Because you're heating up your oven for the roasting, you might as well roast at least four or five beets, saving the rest for another use. Eat this with your favorite bread.*

# TOMATO, BEET, and PEACH STACKS

Preheat the oven to 425°F.

Trim off the beet greens and reserve them. Coat the beet in oil, wrap in foil, and set on a rimmed baking sheet. Bake until tender when you pierce through the foil with a fork, about 1 hour (or longer if the beet is large). Remove from the oven, and let the beet cool. When it's cool enough to handle, slip the skin off with your fingers. Cut the beet into 1/2-inch slices.

Wash and dry the beet greens, then stack, roll, and thinly slice them. Scatter them on a serving dish, drizzle with a little vinaigrette, and make the stacks: Starting with the largest pieces from the middle of the peach, tomato, and beet, and working your way toward the smaller pieces, make three or four stacks that alternate between tomato, peach, and beet slices. Drizzle a little vinaigrette on each slice as you go, crumble the feta on top of each completed stack, and eat.

1 small beet, preferably with its beautiful greens intact

Olive or vegetable oil

2 or 3 tablespoons Walnut Oregano Vinaigrette (page 30)

1 small peach, halved, pitted and cut into 1/2-inch slices

1 medium tomato, cored and cut into 1/2-inch slices

2 tablespoons feta, crumbled

*I was preparing to make an oregano vinaigrette for a salad that was to include toasted walnuts, and I looked at the ingredients and thought, "Why not?" The whole batch of walnuts went into the blender instead of a mixing bowl. The result was a dressing that was richer and creamier than ever. Use this in Tomato, Beet, and Peach Stacks (page 29) or on any vegetable or salad where walnuts would be at home: roasted beets and feta, blanched or roasted green beans, watermelon and tomato, boiled eggs.*

# WALNUT OREGANO VINAIGRETTE

## MAKES ABOUT 1 CUP

Sprinkle the walnuts into a small skillet over medium-high heat. Cook, shaking the pan frequently, until the nuts start to brown and become fragrant. Immediately transfer them to a plate to cool; if you leave them to cool in the pan, they can burn.

When they are cool, combine the walnuts with all the remaining ingredients in a blender, cover, and puree until smooth. (Or use an immersion blender fitted with a jar.) Pour into a glass jar, screw on a lid, and store in the refrigerator for up to 2 weeks.

$1/2$ cup raw walnut halves

$1/3$ cup extra-virgin olive oil

$1/3$ cup red wine vinegar

2 tablespoons fresh oregano leaves

1 clove garlic, chopped

1 teaspoon honey

$1/2$ teaspoon kosher salt

*All good cooks know the truth: recipes evolve. When I wrote Serve Yourself, I was excited to find a recipe for one of my favorite, most memorable salad dressings: a blending of parsley, garlic, and tofu—a dressing I first had at the Japanese restaurant Latacarta when I lived in Peterborough, New Hampshire, seemingly a lifetime ago. It struck me as something of a vegan take on green goddess dressing. Well, it only took a bumper crop of basil to make me realize that this would be even better with a more flavorful herb, which led me to change lemon juice to lime and rice vinegar to apple cider vinegar. Even a goddess, it turns out, has room for improvement. You can take it in other directions, too, substituting other herbs, other oils, other citrus, as long as you keep the proportions the same. This is a natural on height-of-summer tomatoes, or anywhere you want something basil-packed. When you have company, it makes an excellent dip for a platter of crudités; just blend in a slice or two of bread to thicken it, if desired.*

# BASIL GODDESS DRESSING

**MAKES ABOUT 2 CUPS**

Combine all the ingredients in a blender or the bowl of a food processor and blend until smooth. Refrigerate in an airtight container for up to 2 weeks.

1 **(12-ounce) block soft silken tofu, drained**

1 **large or 2 small cloves garlic**

1 **cup lightly packed fresh basil leaves**

2 **tablespoons freshly squeezed lime juice (from 1 lime)**

¼ **cup apple cider vinegar**

¼ **cup extra-virgin olive oil**

1 **teaspoon kosher salt**

*Like the best dressings, this is good on so much more than greens: drizzle it on roasted sweet potatoes, brush it onto broiled eggplant, or toss it with cold soba or udon noodles. Use it to marinate mushrooms before grilling them to make Juicy Bella (page 53). Look for miso paste in the refrigerated section of natural foods stores and Asian markets. If you can find South River brand, made in Massachusetts, snap it up: it's the best I've tasted outside Japan.*

# SESAME MISO VINAIGRETTE

**MAKES ABOUT 1 CUP**

Sprinkle the sesame seeds into a small skillet over medium heat. Cook, shaking the pan frequently, until the sesame seeds have darkened and become fragrant, just a few minutes. Immediately transfer them to a plate to cool; if you leave them to cool in the pan, they can burn.

Use a fork to whisk the miso and sesame oil in a small jar fitted with a lid until smooth. Add the vinegar, vegetable oil, sesame seeds, and honey, close the lid tightly, and vigorously shake to emulsify the dressing. Taste and add more honey if desired, plus salt, and shake again. Store it in the refrigerator for up to 2 weeks.

1  tablespoon sesame seeds

2  tablespoons white miso

2  tablespoons toasted sesame oil

1/2  cup rice vinegar, preferably unseasoned

6  tablespoons neutral vegetable oil, such as canola

2  to 3 teaspoons honey

Sea salt

---

**TIP**

To measure the honey with less mess, first dip the teaspoon into sesame oil, and let the excess drip off. The honey will then slide out easily.

---

*Since I love pungent foods, Japanese umeboshi plum paste has become one of my go-to condiments. Made from ume, a fruit that is more closely related to apricots than plums, umeboshi are little wrinkled, pickled flavor bombs. I tend to mash or puree them before using, so now I just buy the paste from companies such as Eden Foods in natural foods stores and Japanese brands in Asian markets. I use this on many salads, but especially like it on spicy radishes and stirred into rice.*

# SOUR PLUM VINAIGRETTE

**MAKES ABOUT 1 CUP**

Combine all the ingredients in a small glass jar, screw on the lid, and shake to combine. Store in the refrigerator for up to 2 weeks.

- 1/2 cup unseasoned rice vinegar
- 1/4 cup toasted sesame oil
- 2 tablespoons umeboshi plum paste
- 2 tablespoons honey

# FORGET THE CLOCK, REMEMBER YOUR FOOD

*If we were taught to cook as we are taught to walk, encouraged first to feel for pebbles with our toes, then to wobble forward and fall, then had our hands firmly tugged on so we would try again, we would learn that being good at it relies on something deeply rooted, akin to walking, to get good at which we need only guidance, senses, and a little faith.*

**—TAMAR ADLER,** *An Everlasting Meal*, 2011

Things were not going smoothly, not from the host's perspective anyway. It was a summertime dinner party; several of us were sitting on the back deck near the gas grill, and she was scrambling around trying to make sure everybody had a glass of wine or a cocktail or a beer while she also tried to get the food on the table. Judging from the look on her face as she rushed out onto the deck carrying a platter of cut-up chicken, opened the preheated grill, plopped the pieces onto the grates, shut the lid, and set the timer, I realized that she was in the state restaurant cooks refer to as "in the weeds."

She looked around to see who might help her check this item off her punch list. I was just about to offer when she looked at me, perhaps sensing my sympathy, and asked: "Could you turn these over when the timer goes off?"

"I'd be glad to take over the chicken, sure thing," I said.

That wasn't what she meant. She sighed. "This is a *Cook's Illustrated* recipe," she said with a little irritation in her voice. "And they

say to turn them after 12 minutes, so when the timer goes off, would you just turn them?"

My mother raised me to be polite, so I wasn't about to argue with her—not out loud, anyway. In my head, I was running through all sorts of smart-alecky replies, such as, "I seriously doubt the *Cook's* recipe said that boneless chicken breasts, bone-in leg/thigh combinations, and little wings would all be done at the same time, and I doubt it said that the chicken breasts should be cut in such different-sized pieces, and I doubt it didn't give you any ways to tell the chicken would be ready to turn other than the timing." Or, "I know Chris Kimball, and, madam, you're no Chris Kimball."

Instead, I said, "Of course, no problem," and then as soon as she was back in the house, I turned off the timer. Sure enough, some of the smaller pieces were ready for flipping in just a few minutes, some of the bigger ones took a little longer, and still others—those leg-and-thigh combos—took the longest. I listened for their sizzle, I looked at the color, I felt them for firmness, I checked the juices, and I switched them around to parts of the grill that were cooler and hotter, depending on what I thought they needed. I took them off as they were ready, and kept them warm under a loose tent of foil. The host was too busy with other duties to notice my rebellion.

The venerable author and cooking teacher Anne Willan, who has been writing recipes for fifty years, tells a similar tale. "My recent trainees and even my current assistant cannot understand that timing, especially on baking, is approximate and you must keep in communication all the time with what you are cooking," she wrote me in an email when I reached out to her on the subject. "It drives me crackers!" Later, when we talked by phone, she elaborated. Her assistants "do this thing of putting on the timer, going away, looking at their computer or making phone calls. And then I say, 'That's going to be nearly done, I think.' I've developed an instinct for some things that it's nearly there. 'Oh, no,' they'll say. 'The timer hasn't gone, it's still 5 more minutes.' They think anything written down has got to be followed exactly, and it's quite difficult to get across that every time is a little bit different."

I've never really been like that in the kitchen, and I think it comes from having learned to cook my first dishes not from a cookbook but from my mother and stepfather when I was a kid. When my mom taught me how to whip cream using her stand mixer, for instance, she would caution me to keep stopping and checking the thickness—and to be careful not to whip it so long it would turn to butter. I had my own ideas, at age eight, of what thick whipped cream should

be like—like Cool Whip, of course!—so I was confident in pushing past the point where she would have stopped. Similarly, in my stepdad's lesson on making chicken-fried steak, he showed me how to tell from the color of the crust when to turn each piece, and how it wouldn't be done in the middle if the juices were running red.

Hang out with any good home cook or professional chef, and you'll see less clock-watching and more poking and prodding, sniffing and tasting, and even listening, as they evaluate the food as it progresses and guide it along the way. (Sous vide cooking, which uses vacuum packs, is one exception, which is one reason I've resisted it.) I remember shadowing baker Renee McLeod at her Petsi Pies café in Cambridge, Massachusetts, one morning many years ago, and there was no timer in sight. Instead, right in the middle of answering one of my questions, her nose went into the air and she sniffed, then whirled around to her convection oven and pulled out a tray of coconut cupcakes, which were perfectly done—by a matter of mere seconds. She doesn't have to be in such close proximity, either. She told me, "I'll be sitting in the office and suddenly I'll call out to my people, 'Cookies are done!'"

Some people's senses seem born stronger than others', of course, but there's no doubt that much of this kind of skill comes from experience. McLeod adapted some of her cupcake recipes from her grandmother's instructions for larger cakes, which means that the first time she made them she would have had no idea how long they would take. She had to watch, sniff, and learn. In a professional setting like McLeod's, where recipes are standardized as they are made over and over again using the same equipment, and the equipment is professionally calibrated, the variability lessens and timing can become more consistent. But ovens can rarely be calibrated to within 25 degrees, and most home ovens are far more inaccurate than that. Moreover, when you're following someone else's instructions—someone who was using different ingredients and equipment—it's folly to depend solely on the clock rather than learning to evaluate your food and make adjustments as you go.

Take the simple sautéed onion. It's all too common for recipe writers to tell readers how long it will take to get it tender, along with that garlic or carrot or celery that might also be in the skillet. But an onion is not an onion is not an onion. Even if a "large" onion is called for and used, the actual size will vary; and it could be younger or older than it was last time, meaning juicier or tougher. And even if you call for a medium or large skillet, one person's medium is another person's large, and a heavy cast-iron one is not the same as a thin aluminum one, especially when the onion actually starts cooking. Sure, a writer can try to specify as many of those variables as possible—the number of cups the chopped onion should be, the exact size of the pan, even its materials—but who knows the age of an onion, unless you grow it yourself? All those factors will affect the cooking time, and yet too many writers, even as we acknowledge the variables, act like the timing is the one thing we can specify with some certainty.

Onions, as it happens, were the subject of some scorn heaped on recipe writers last spring, when Tom Scocca wrote a piece in *Slate* about the woefully short time so many recipes say it takes to caramelize an onion, something that, when done properly, can occupy the better part of an hour—or more. But as Chow .com editor John Birdsall wrote in response, "The thing that went mostly unnoticed in the scramble to accuse or save face was Scocca's larger indictment, which is that professional recipe writers' work can seem as far removed from actual cooking as a cognitive study in the testing lab with subjects wired to electrodes is from actual thinking. Recipe writing occurs under unnatural conditions, conducted by professionals with laptops and clipboards. They pretend they're doing stuff that ordinary home cooks might do, but they're not ordinary home cooks, and many are definitely not cooking at home, under ordinary conditions."

It was not always thus. In her fascinating book *The Cookbook Library*, Willan says that it wasn't until the twentieth century that writers started regularly listing precise timing, mostly because until then most cooks had wood stoves with no consistency of temperature whatsoever. Cooks would test the heat of wood stoves using their hands, or they would put in some newspaper and see how long it took the paper to scorch: thirty seconds was very hot and good for baking pastries, for instance, then as the temperature came down it was appropriate for bread, then roasts, then stews. "In Catholic countries, they would time it by saying a rosary," Willan says. "And of course if the paper didn't brown or scorch at all, then the oven wasn't hot enough for anything." Even when she went to Le Cordon Bleu in Paris in the 1960s, the equipment was so antiquated as to make timing estimates pointless. "The ovens had top heat, bottom heat or both together, and we controlled the heat by putting a wooden spoon in the door, propping it open," she said.

Exceptions to Willan's twentieth-century observation abound, naturally. Fannie Farmer's *The Boston Cooking School Cook-Book* of 1895 is largely credited with introducing specific measurements, times, and temperatures to recipe writing. When I scoured through some other antiquarian books, I noticed that *The Improved Housewife* of 1846 would include timing in one recipe and not in the next. For parsnips and carrots, you just "boil till tender," but for beets that same instruction is followed by "in summer one hour, in winter three." Don Lindgren, co-owner of Rabelais Books in Biddeford, Maine, says that even Mary Randolph included some timing in her influential 1825 book, *The Virginia House-Wife*. But the most entertaining outlier I saw was an excerpt from *The Nonpareil Cook Book*, an 1894 collection by the Ladies' Lend-A-Hand Society of the Baptist Church of Worcester, New York, that Lindgren sent me. The book includes a chart for vegetable boiling times that by today's standards are comical, including a half-hour for potatoes, an hour for squash, three hours for string beans, and four hours for beets. (The latter in winter, I presume.)

Ultimately, recipe writing, like so many other things, is an idiosyncratic discipline, with writers taking all sorts of approaches in getting across their own interpretations of a dish, and teaching it in their own style. To this day, charcoal grilling calls for an approach similar to the rosaries Willan mentioned;

many Southern recipes instruct cooks to count how many "Mississippis" they can utter while holding their hand over the grate, while many of those same recipes still attempt to say how many minutes it then takes to char an eggplant. In a recipe for baked red snapper with grapefruit in *The New York Times Cookbook* of 1961, Craig Claiborne wisely leaves out the minutes it takes to accomplish of one of the first, most basic steps: "In a skillet heat four tablespoons of the butter, add the onion and cook until it is transparent." My style exactly. And then he specifies that the stuffed fish should be baked "until it flakes easily when tested with a fork, about fifty to sixty minutes," a crucial step for which he gives the reader a good testing mechanism. By 1979, though, his friend and frequent coauthor, Pierre Franey, was going in the opposite direction in his *60-Minute Gourmet*, deemphasizing descriptive cues and listing a time whenever possible. It makes sense; as more and more women were leaving domestic life behind in favor of the workplace, our cooking culture was becoming ever more focused on speed and convenience. Perhaps Franey's approach was to some degree a way of helping readers count the minutes and see for themselves that they wouldn't add up to more than the all-important hour he was promising.

After a long downward trend in home cooking, recent years have seen a rediscovery of the kitchen. That's nothing but good news. Yet the standards are different when the target audience includes less experienced cooks, and trying to account for this is where I think we've started to really go off the rails with recipe timing. When I called Sally

Schneider, author of *The Improvisational Cook*, to talk about the issue, she said that as much as she tries to write recipes that include many other descriptive cues in addition to timing, she still gets emails and calls from readers asking shockingly basic questions, such as how to tell when that simple sautéed onion is done: "The problem is people these days don't have basic structures in place in their heads."

Writers and editors often think that to make recipes doable by less experienced cooks, they must attach time cues to each and every step, however small, and to weigh or otherwise measure every last smidgen of every last ingredient. The irony, though, is that by trying to account for so many variables, the recipes can become so long-winded that they run the risk of intimidating the very cooks they're trying to appeal to. Even worse, they might be doing a disservice by not helping even the most inexperienced cooks learn what I think they need to learn most: How to make their own judgments. How to interact with their food, to roll with the punches, to develop instincts. How to make mistakes, and recover. How to learn. How to be free. Schneider echoes the old "teach a man to fish" adage when she says, "If you tell somebody how something works, if they understand the workings of it and what its end point can be, it gives them more confidence."

Technology has long tried to come to the rescue of home cooks (most of them women) who had their hands full, whether with other household chores or work outside the home. Generations of slow-cooker devotees have loved the fact that they can close the thing up, head to work, and come home to a meal. That Ronco rotisserie oven hawked on TV has sold gazillions on the promise of its earworm of a slogan, shouted out by Ron Popeil and the audience in chorus: "Set it and forget it!"

But should we forget it, really? As Willan said, cooking has always been about multitasking. Nobody's asking you to stand there and do nothing except watch the cake rise in the oven. "But you still have to have it in the back of your mind while you do other things," she said. "It's a skill to be acquired."

I'm no Luddite, but I can't ignore some of the tradeoffs we've made in our dependence on technology. For example, I'm as addicted to my smartphone as anyone I know, and am especially dependent on the built-in GPS to overcome my lack of a natural sense of direction. So when I'm walking or driving and staring at Google Maps rather than at the streetscape around me, I don't really learn where I'm going, I just get there anyway. What's the harm in that, you may ask? Well, putting aside the possibility of running into a parking meter on the sidewalk, or heaven forbid into oncoming traffic, the harm is that this is just one more area where I'm getting a little bit dumber, a little less independent. More than once I've run out of battery before I see where I'm supposed to make a turn, sending me into the nearest gas station or Starbucks to do the old-fashioned thing, and ask for help.

There are countless cooking apps, too, and many feature built-in timers, not to mention voice commands to move from one step in the recipe to the next. Maybe one day Siri will teach everybody to cook, or perhaps she'll do the sautéing herself. But in the meantime, when you're in the kitchen, why not just…

look up? As author Tamar Adler puts it, learning to cook by interacting closely with your food is a little like learning to drive on a stick shift rather than an automatic. You feel more connected to the process of driving, and therefore you understand it a little better.

Adler's book *An Everlasting Meal* calls for a return to instinctive cooking, and she tells audiences and students and readers that they can make their own decisions about recipes, that they don't need to be slaves to any instruction, timing included. And she says they are surprisingly quick to respond. "At first they feel incredibly unmoored and unsupported, and they say, 'That's all well and good for you, because you know how long everything takes, and the processes, so you're not nervous, but what about me?' I always say, 'I learned this by standing over the pan and paying attention.'"

When you read this book, and cook from it, I want you to pay attention, and also to make its contents your own. You may have heard this before, but I'm going to say it again: Recipes—mine and everyone's—are road maps. Throw away the stone-tablets idea, and you'll eventually be a better cook.

The more I think about this issue, the more committed I become to making sure my own recipes give readers something more than just a bunch of numbers. I have long insisted that my own recipes in the *Washington Post*

put the time cue last in a sequence, the hope being that if readers read that the eggplant should be baked "until it blackens and collapses, about an hour," rather than the other way around, they'll be more attuned to the blackening and collapsing part of the equation. When I initially sent the recipes for this book to testers, I asked for feedback on the plethora of time references, to make sure as much as possible that the ranges I was giving were working for others, and I used that feedback to make sure they did. But then I made another decision: in many of the instructions, particularly the ones about sautéing an onion or anything else that happens relatively quickly—and exceedingly variably—the time references have come out altogether. In their place, I'm trying to describe to you as best I can how to tell what's happening with the food and, therefore, how to really cook it.

The result, I hope, is that you might find your own cooking rhythms and realize the point of all this: that what you see, hear, smell, and feel happening is the only thing that matters. I think it might be easier for single cooks to get there than others. If your primary consideration is your own craving and nobody else's, you can learn more naturally to listen to your instincts as you cook, and to let them lead the way—hopefully to something that satisfies you. No matter how long those onions took to soften.

## Chapter 2

# SANDWICHES and SOUPS

The sandwich, in one form or another, might be the most intuitive single-serving dish there is. Once you've got your bread slices, it's pretty easy to imagine what might fit between them that would satisfy you. Because vegetables aren't quite as convenient as cold cuts from the deli, you may have to do a little more cooking and employ a little more creativity than a carnivore might, but the resulting sandwich can be even more interesting. For the most part, what I want from a good sammie is this: something rich, something salty, something crunchy, and something tart. Maybe something spicy, too.

Of course, the bread is key. (Isn't it always?) Whether it's a pillowy pita or slices from a soft pullman, sourdough, multigrain loaf, or buttery brioche, make it fresh (or freshly defrosted) and, when possible, from a great artisan baker. Really good bread is worth seeking out.

Soups, on the other hand, might just be the least intuitive thing for us solo cooks, perhaps because as soon as things start going into the pot it's all too easy to keep adding, adding, adding—everybody in the pool!—without holding on to a good idea of the quantity that's resulting. Before you know it you've got enough for a party, which is a good thing—if you're having a party. Instead, it takes a little practice (or the right recipes) to learn how to downscale. If you still can't get the hang of it, and you'd rather make bigger quantities of soup and freeze the leftovers for later, I won't blame you.

*Veggie burgers have gotten better as demand for meatless options has increased, but in the freezer aisles of supermarkets and on the menus of restaurants you still find dry, bland, or mushy disks that not even a staunch vegetarian can embrace. Many seem to contain precious little evidence of what makes them what they are: vegetables. And others are often as mushy as bean dip, because that's pretty much what they are. I think I fixed all that by packing this homemade version with mushrooms, peas, and intact beans, which I bake before pan-frying to give the patties a firm, chunky texture. Veggie burgers are one thing you should make in larger quantities, since they freeze so well and you'll be glad you have them around. After baking but before frying, wrap each one in plastic wrap and stack them in ziplock bags to freeze (see "A Vacuum Shortcut," page 171). When you want one (or more), just thaw and finish in a frying pan—or, naturally, on the grill. I've used all kinds of beans with these, but chickpeas are my favorite for their starchy texture. These are excellent when the buns are spread with a little mayo mixed, or pureed, with Quick-Pickled Golden Raisins (page 172).*

# CURRIED MUSHROOM BEAN BURGERS

### MAKES EIGHT 4-INCH BURGERS

Pour the olive oil into a large skillet over medium heat, and when the oil shimmers, add the onion, garlic, and one or both jalapeños, depending on how spicy you want these. Cook, stirring occasionally, until the vegetables are tender and lightly browned. Sprinkle in the curry powder, stir to combine, and let the mixture sizzle briefly, then stir in the mushrooms and peas. Cook, stirring occasionally, until the mushrooms collapse. Transfer to a large bowl and let cool to room temperature.

Whisk together the miso and vinegar in a bowl, then add to mushrooms. Mash the beans very lightly with a fork, then stir them into the bowl. Taste and season generously with salt, then vigorously stir in the flour until it is thoroughly combined. Cover, and chill in the refrigerator until the filling is firm, at least 2 hours.

Use a little of the vegetable oil to lightly oil a baking sheet, and preheat the oven to 375°F. Remove the burger mixture from the refrigerator. Use your hands to form it into 8 patties. If the mixture is too sticky to work with easily, fill a bowl with water, dipping your hands in it between making patties. Place the patties on the baking sheet and bake for 20 minutes, then turn

1   tablespoon extra-virgin olive oil

1   medium onion, chopped

3   cloves garlic, chopped

1   or 2 jalapeños, stemmed, seeded, and chopped

2   teaspoons curry powder

1   pound oyster mushrooms, chopped (may substitute cremini, button, or shiitake mushrooms)

1/2   cup fresh or thawed frozen peas

1   tablespoon white miso

1   tablespoon unseasoned rice vinegar

1   cup cooked and lightly drained beans, preferably homemade (page 175); may substitute low-sodium canned, thoroughly rinsed and drained

Sea salt

1   cup all-purpose flour

Vegetable oil

them over and keep baking until they are firm, very dry on top, and golden brown on the edges, another 10 to 15 minutes. If you're not using them all right away, cool them to room temperature before refrigerating or freezing.

When ready to serve the burgers, pour vegetable oil to a depth of 1/4 inch in a large skillet. Pan-fry the burgers until nicely browned and crisp on each side. Drain them on a paper towel–lined plate or a cooling rack set over a plate.

Serve the burgers with your favorite condiments on hamburger buns.

---

*Since I tend to cook most meals from scratch, I don't often use packaged meat substitutes, but the products have gotten better and better over the years, and I've found some favorites. I like to make this vegan version of my namesake sandwich whenever I get my hands on chorizo-style "sausage" or seitan made by Field Roast or Upton's Naturals, respectively.*

# SLOPPY VEGAN JOE

Pour the olive oil into a skillet over medium heat. When it shimmers, add the onion and garlic and sauté until they soften. Stir in the red pepper flakes and the seitan, and cook until it's warmed through. Add the cherry tomatoes and squash and cook until the tomatoes collapse. Taste and add salt as needed. Reduce the heat to medium-low, cover, and continue cooking until the squash is tender but not mushy.

Pile the mixture onto the bun or in the pocket of the pita, top with the pickle slices, and eat.

1 tablespoon extra-virgin olive oil

1 small onion, chopped

1 clove garlic, chopped

1/4 teaspoon crushed red pepper flakes (optional)

1/2 cup chorizo-spiced seitan or other vegan meat, crumbled or cut into 1/4-inch pieces

8 large cherry tomatoes, quartered

1 small yellow squash, cut into 1/2-inch pieces

Sea salt

1 hamburger bun or soft pita, warmed

1 medium sour pickle, thinly sliced

*After Kimchi Deviled Eggs (page 146), this sandwich was my second foray into using the Korean staple to liven up American comfort foods. Since its punch reminded me of the pimento in the classic Southern cheese dip, I thought, why not try it in a sandwich with cheese? So simple, so perfect. The play between spicy, crunchy kimchi, sharp cheese, and sweet pear has made this one of my go-to meals whenever my fridge is emptier than usual. Omnivores, the sandwich also takes nicely to the addition of a little ham, but it's gorgeous without it.*

# GRILLED KIMCHEESE

Brush the bread slices with oil on one side. Layer the bare (nonoiled) side of one slice with cheese, kimchi, and pear slices. Drizzle with a little Sriracha if you want the sandwich to be particularly spicy. Top with the other bread slice, unoiled side facing in, and press with your hand to flatten.

Set a medium skillet over medium heat for a few minutes, then lay the sandwich in the pan and cook, pressing with a spatula from time to time, until the underside is golden brown and the cheese starts to melt. Repeat on the other side, transfer to a plate, and eat.

2 slices multigrain sandwich bread

2 teaspoons vegetable oil

1/4 cup grated sharp cheddar cheese

1/4 cup Cabbage Kimchi (page 163) or spicy store-bought kimchi, drained and chopped

1/4 to 1/2 small Asian pear, cored and thinly sliced

Sriracha (optional)

*This is for those times when I want a PBJ but want to cook a little bit, too. The realization came when I bought an expensive (but delicious) plum spread to pair with almond butter and realized that it tasted like little more than pureed prunes. I always have prunes around, so I scratched the plum spread off my regular shopping list. For more ideas of nut butter and dried fruit combinations, see page 47. Note: This recipe gives you enough plum spread for two sandwiches. Why? Because any less would require a mini food processor. If you have one, feel free to cut that part of the recipe in half.*

# GRILLED ALMOND BUTTER and DRIED PLUM SANDWICH

Combine the prunes, orange zest, and juice in the bowl of a food processor and puree until a chunky spread forms. Taste and add a touch of honey if you'd like it to be a little sweeter.

Brush one side of each piece of bread with the oil. Spread the almond butter and plum spread on the unoiled sides of the bread slices, and press together to form the sandwich.

Heat a small skillet over medium-high heat and grill the sandwich until golden brown on both sides.

9  **large pitted prunes**

**Grated zest and juice of 1 orange (about 2 tablespoons each)**

**Honey (optional)**

2  **slices brioche or challah**

1  **teaspoon vegetable oil**

2  **tablespoons almond butter**

# More Nut Butter and Dried Fruit Sandwich Ideas

It's hard to go wrong with the combination of nut butter and dried fruit, especially if you turn the latter into a spread so you're not biting into a chewy chunk when you're eating the otherwise gooey sandwich. Nut butters are easier than ever to find in good grocery stores (and through such online sources as Fastachi, page 181), but you can also make your own with a food processor and a little patience.

For best results, start with raw nuts and toast them yourself, then puree them while they're still warm. Let them go for several minutes, and they will eventually turn from powder to paste, but if you get impatient drizzle in a neutral vegetable oil, which should get them going in the right direction.

Once you've got the nut butter, here are some other sandwich possibilities using dried fruit spreads. For the latter, puree in a food processor, adding the liquid a little at a time until you like the taste. My favorites:

Pecan butter + peach spread (dried peaches, lime juice and zest)

Pistachio butter + cherry spread (dried cherries, lemon juice and zest)

Hazelnut butter + fig spread (dried figs, balsamic vinegar)

Walnut or cashew butter + date spread (dates, pomegranate molasses)

*Why not put the "grilled" back into a grilled cheese sandwich? This does that—but there's much more than cheese on this baby. You single folks can make the most of a small grill by charring the poblano chile while the grill is hot, cooking the mushrooms over medium heat, then grilling the sandwich. But it's also an easy recipe to double for a companion or multiply (on a larger grill) for a crowd, or for leftovers. King oyster mushrooms are my favorite for this preparation, because they are so meaty and take to grilling so well, but you can substitute portobellos if desired.*

# GRILLED MUSHROOM, POBLANO, and CHEESE SANDWICH

Whisk together the mustard, vinegar, and oil in a medium bowl until emulsified. Add the mushroom slices and toss to coat evenly. Let them marinate for 15 to 30 minutes while you prepare the grill and char the poblano.

Prepare the grill for direct heat. If using a gas grill, preheat to high (650°F). If using a charcoal grill, light the charcoal or wood briquettes; when the briquettes are almost completely covered in white ash, mound them in the center of the grill. For a very hot fire, you should be able to hold your hand about 6 inches above the coals for 1 or 2 seconds. Have ready a spray water bottle for taming flames. Lightly coat the grill rack with oil and place it on the grill.

Grill the poblano, turning it every few minutes, until it is charred on all sides, about 10 minutes total. Transfer to a small bowl and cover tightly with plastic wrap.

If using a gas grill, reduce the heat to medium-high (450°F). If using a charcoal grill, carefully remove the grill rack and spread the coals into an even layer, carefully removing some if necessary to achieve a medium-hot fire; you should be able to hold your hand about 6 inches above the coals for 4 or 5 seconds.

Remove the mushroom slices from the marinade and grill them until deeply browned, about 5 minutes per side. Transfer to a cutting board to cool, then chop them into bite-size pieces.

When the charred poblano is cool enough to handle, use your fingers to slip off the blackened skin (resist the urge to rinse the pepper, which would remove too much flavor), then

1 teaspoon Dijon mustard

2 teaspoons red wine vinegar

2 teaspoons extra-virgin olive oil

4 ounces king oyster mushrooms or portobellos, cut lengthwise into 1/4-inch slices

1 medium poblano chile

2 slices rustic wheat bread

1 1/2 ounces Gruyère or other melting cheese, sliced thin (about 3 tablespoons)

1 medium dill pickle, sliced thin

discard the stem, tear open the pepper, and scoop out and discard the seeds. Cut the pepper into bite-size strips.

If you have any marinade left, brush it on one side of each slice of bread. With the brushed side facing down, layer one slice of the bread with half of the cheese, followed by the mushroom pieces, poblano, pickle slices, and the rest of the cheese. Top with the other bread slice (brushed side facing up), and press the sandwich with your hand to flatten it.

Grill the sandwich until the bread is golden brown and the cheese melts, 2 to 4 minutes per side. Transfer to a plate, cut in half, and eat.

*Vegetable lovers deserve hearty sandwiches just as much as meatheads, don't you think? After you taste this one, with its smoke-kissed cabbage, flavor-packed tofu, and pungent tapenade, you may have a hard time going back to veggie wraps. I love the sandwich technique I learned about in Tom Colicchio's 'wichcraft book: toasting just one side of the bread, and assembling the sandwich with that side facing in, so you get the crunch on the inside but bite into the softer side first. These sandwich fillings are also delicious rolled in rice paper wrappers for a cross-cultural version of a spring roll.*

# TOFU, GRILLED CABBAGE, and POBLANO TAPENADE SANDWICH

Lay the bread on a work surface with the toasted sides facing up. Spread the poblano tapenade on one piece of bread, and top with the grilled cabbage and the tofu slices. Spread the mayonnaise on the other piece of bread, invert it onto the sandwich, slice it in half, and eat.

2 slices sourdough bread, toasted on one side

2 tablespoons Poblano Tapenade (page 151) or store-bought tapenade mixed with chopped fresh jalapeño

$1/2$ cup chopped Grilled Cabbage (page 165)

$1/2$ cup Marinated and Baked Tofu (page 170) or store-bought baked tofu, sliced $1/4$ inch thick

1 tablespoon mayonnaise

*This is a gooey, cheesy sandwich, a marriage of garlic-spiked chickpeas and already braised greens—and with a little punch of something extra. For those of you who are saying, "What the heck are Peppadews?" I'm so glad you asked, because it gives me a chance to spread the word. This brand of jarred sweet-and-sour-and-a-touch-spicy miniature peppers from South Africa is one of my favorite ways to add oomph to a sandwich. Chop or blend them up into the mayo or mustard or, in this case, just add them to the layers. They also make a great addition to a cheese plate or pickle tray. Look for them near the olives and pickles in supermarkets; some markets sell them by weight in olive bars.*

# GRILLED GREENS, CHICKPEA, and PEPPADEW SANDWICH

In a small bowl, combine the chickpeas, garlic, and 2 teaspoons of the olive oil. Lightly smash the chickpeas with a fork, leaving the mixture chunky. Taste and season generously with salt and several grinds of black pepper.

Put a medium skillet over medium heat. Brush one side of each piece of bread with the remaining teaspoon of olive oil. Put one piece oiled side down on your work surface, and top with half the cheese, followed by the greens, the chickpea mixture, the Peppadews, and the remaining half of the cheese. Top with the other piece of bread, with the oiled side facing out. Press lightly with your palm to slightly compress the sandwich.

Transfer the sandwich to the skillet and cook it until the cheese has melted and the bread is lightly browned and crisp. Transfer it to a plate, cut in half, and eat.

- $1/3$ **cup cooked chickpeas, preferably homemade (page 175), rinsed if canned, drained**
- 1 **clove garlic, minced**
- 1 **tablespoon extra-virgin olive oil**

  **Sea salt**

  **Freshly ground black pepper**
- 2 **slices multigrain sandwich bread**
- $1/4$ **cup shredded or chopped fontina**
- $1/3$ **cup cooked greens, drained (page 173)**
- 3 **Peppadews, drained and chopped**

*As a cookbook author, one of the best emails I can hope for starts with something along the lines of "I have a great recipe for you." This one came from my friend and former colleague Jane Black. She had just eaten a sandwich at 606 R&D (in Prospect Heights, Brooklyn) that was notable for one quality: it could make even Jane, a notorious zucchini hater, like the vegetable. The key is ricotta, good ricotta, and lots of it. Well, I'm not a zucchini hater by any means, but spread three-quarters of an inch of good ricotta on any sandwich and I'll bite. She didn't give me an actual recipe, but described the sandwich to a T, so who needed one? When I made it— with my homemade Whipped Ricotta (page 153)—I had new proof that if the ingredients are just right, the simplest recipes can be the most satisfying.*

# RICOTTA, ZUCCHINI, and RADICCHIO SANDWICH

Preheat the oven broiler with the rack set 4 to 5 inches from the flame or element. Toast the bread under the broiler until it's deep golden brown on just one side, 1 to 2 minutes. Transfer to a plate.

Spread the toasted side of one slice of bread with all but a tablespoon of the ricotta. Use a vegetable peeler to cut the zucchini into paper-thin slices, and lay them on the ricotta, sprinkling each layer with a little lemon juice, salt, and pepper. Top with the radicchio and shallot.

Spread the remaining tablespoon of ricotta on the toasted side of the second piece of bread, turn the toasted side down, and top the sandwich with it. Cut in half and eat.

2 thick slices pullman or other soft white bread

$^1/_3$ to $^1/_2$ cup Whipped Ricotta (page 153)

1 very small or $^1/_2$ medium zucchini

2 tablespoons freshly squeezed lemon juice

Sea salt

Freshly ground black pepper

3 or 4 radicchio leaves, stacked and thinly sliced

1 small shallot, thinly sliced

*You know the Juicy Lucy, right? It's a cheese-stuffed burger that was born in Minneapolis in the 1950s, and legend has it that it got its name when the first patron took a bite and exclaimed, "That's one juicy lucy!" Well, my friend Erin Meister, who blogs as The Nervous Cook, sent me her take on it: a marinated portobello mushroom cap stuffed with a runny-yolk egg. A total umami bomb and, like the Juicy Lucy, a mess to eat. But when you're cooking for yourself, who cares if you have egg on your face? Erin marinates the mushroom in a miso-vinegar mixture, but since I usually have Sesame Miso Vinaigrette (page 32) on hand, it's perfect to use here, too. If you don't have it, substitute 1 tablespoon of white miso in 3 tablespoons of rice vinegar. If you don't have a grill, you won't get the smoky tinge, but this works just fine inside, using a cast-iron skillet or grill pan fitted with a lid (or aluminum foil).*

# JUICY BELLA

Turn the mushroom cap stem side up. To make room for the egg, use a spoon to gently scrape out the dark brown gills from the underside of the cap, and discard them. Pour the vinaigrette over the mushroom in a shallow bowl and let it marinate for at least 15 minutes. Turn the mushroom a time or two in the marinade.

Meanwhile, preheat a gas grill to medium heat or build a small fire in a charcoal grill; the coals will be ready when they have burned down to smoldering and are covered in white ash, and you can hold your hand 4 inches above the grill for no more than 4 seconds. Clean the grates and brush them with oil. Grill the onion rounds on both sides until they are deeply browned and starting to collapse. Transfer to a plate to cool.

Grill the mushroom cap gill side down until deeply browned, just a few minutes. (Watch it carefully to make sure it doesn't burn.) Turn it over, and carefully crack an egg into the mushroom cup. Sprinkle it lightly with salt, close the grill, and cook just until the white has set but the yolk is still runny, another few minutes. Transfer to the plate.

If desired, grill the bun or pita halves lightly on both sides. Spread the mustard on one of the bun halves, top with lettuce, grilled onion, egg-stuffed mushroom, and the other bun, and eat.

1 **very large portobello mushroom cap (5 or 6 inches in diameter), stem removed**

1/4 **cup Sesame Miso Vinaigrette (page 32)**

1 **very small onion, cut into 1/2-inch rounds**

1 **large egg**

**Sea salt**

1 **hamburger bun or soft pita, split**

1 **tablespoon spicy mustard**

**Lettuce**

*I was rooting around in the fridge, desperately hungry to make a quick lunch, and here's what I turned up: a bunch of kale, sweet caramelized onions, grated mozzarella left over from a top-your-own-pizza party, corn tortillas I had made the day before, and various jars of salsa (including my own salsa verde from my first cookbook, Serve Yourself). What would you do? Yep. That's what I did, too.*

# KALE and CARAMELIZED ONION QUESADILLA

Wash and very thoroughly dry the kale leaves, then thinly slice them. In a medium bowl, toss them with the lime juice, then pick them up by the handful and squeeze, repeating until you have squeezed all the kale and it has turned bright green and wilted. Sprinkle with salt to taste and the cayenne pepper, and toss to combine.

Pour the olive oil into a medium skillet over medium heat. When the oil starts to shimmer, place one of the corn tortillas in the skillet and press it down with a spatula, then sprinkle it with half the cheese and the kale leaves. Top with the caramelized onions, sprinkle with the remaining cheese, and set the other tortilla on top. Press down with the spatula to flatten the quesadilla as it cooks and the kale further collapses.

Cook the quesadilla until it is browned and crisp on the bottom, then gently turn it over and cook it until browned and crisp on the other side. Transfer it to a plate, cut it in quarters, top with salsa, and eat.

1 cup (about 2 ounces) kale leaves, stripped from their stems

2 tablespoons freshly squeezed lime juice (from 1 lime)

Sea salt

Pinch of cayenne pepper

1 tablespoon extra-virgin olive oil

2 (6-inch) corn tortillas

1/4 cup grated mozzarella cheese, preferably smoked

2 tablespoons Caramelized Onions (page 166)

1/2 cup salsa verde or other salsa

*I was almost at the end of a fun afternoon of make-your-own tofu tinkering with cookbook author Andrea Nguyen when she got a twinkle in her eye. "I've got something else to show you," she said. "I think it's perfect for your book." She cut up some tofu, whisked an egg with cornstarch and seasonings, stirred it all together, and quickly fried up these pancakes, which we topped with bean sprouts, herbs, and spicy peanut sauce and ate like lettuce wraps. Perfect indeed, especially since I'm always looking for things to do with leftover tofu. When I make it at home, I turn it from a snack for four people to a main course for me and me alone, and I add another of my favorite ingredients: greens. Feel free to top with whatever seasonal, crunchy produce strikes your fancy.*

# INDONESIAN TOFU and EGG WRAPS

## MAKES 4 WRAPS, TO SERVE 1 AS A MEAL OR 2 AS A SNACK

Cut the tofu into thin, bite-size pieces. In a small bowl, dissolve the cornstarch in 1 teaspoon of water. Whisk in the egg, salt, and pepper, then stir in the tofu.

Pour the oil into a medium skillet, preferably nonstick or well-seasoned cast iron, over medium-high heat. When it shimmers, make the pancakes by spooning a quarter of the egg/tofu mixture (about 2 to 3 tablespoons) into the skillet, laying the tofu pieces down flat if possible. Fry until golden brown on each side, about 1 minute, then fry on the first side again to get it even crispier, about 30 seconds. Transfer to a rack to cool.

Top each pancake with bean sprouts, basil, kale or other greens, and sauce, and eat with your hands.

²/₃ cup Marinated and Baked Tofu (page 170) or store-bought baked or extra-firm tofu, drained

¹/₂ teaspoon cornstarch

1 egg

¹/₄ teaspoon sea salt

¹/₄ teaspoon ground black pepper

1 tablespoon vegetable oil

¹/₂ cup bean sprouts, washed, drained well, and cut into 1-inch pieces

6 large basil leaves

¹/₄ cup massaged kale (see page 22), lettuce, or drained and chopped cooked greens (page 173)

¹/₄ cup store-bought spicy peanut sauce or reserved marinade from Marinated and Baked Tofu (page 170)

*On a hot day, I want a cold pureed soup. This one goes down almost like a green smoothie, but I turn it into a meal by holding out some of the peas, mashing them with feta, and spreading it on thin toast as if it were the world's largest crouton. (There's a fine line between a smoothie and a cold soup; it's mostly a matter of the serving vessel and the garnish, isn't it?) By the way, I don't recommend low-fat or nonfat yogurt here, because the result can be slightly chalky rather than silky.*

# MINTY PEA SOUP with PEA and FETA TOAST

Bring a medium saucepan of salted water to a boil, then blanch the peas until bright green and tender but not mushy, no more than a few minutes. Drain and let cool.

Remove ¼ cup of the peas and combine them in a small bowl with the feta. Drizzle with 1 tablespoon of the olive oil, mash with a fork, and spread on the toast.

Reserve a pinch each of the mint and chives for garnish. Combine the rest with the remaining 1¼ cup of peas, the yogurt, and the remaining 1 tablespoon of olive oil in a blender, add the ice cube, and blend until very smooth and frothy. Add a little water if needed to thin the soup. Taste and add salt as needed. Pour into a bowl, sprinkle with the reserved chopped mint and chives, and eat with the pea and feta toast.

1½ cups freshly shelled English peas (may substitute thawed frozen peas)

2 tablespoons crumbled feta

2 tablespoons extra-virgin olive oil

2 slices baguette or 1 large slice bread, toasted

8 large mint leaves, chopped

¼ cup chopped chives

1 cup plain whole-milk Greek-style yogurt

1 ice cube

Sea salt

*I tasted the original version of this soup at El Naranjo, the fabulous Austin restaurant owned by Ileana and Ernesto de la Vega, back when they were serving out of a trailer. I immediately scratched down my thoughts on the intense combination of sweet, salty, and spicy flavors, asked them for the recipe—and then messed with it, as is my way. I scaled it down, added a little tofu to turn it from an appetizer into a meal, and made the executive decision to substitute Asian pear for the jicama root, since the two remind me so much of each other in texture but the pear adds a touch of sweetness.*

# COOL, SPICY MANGO YOGURT SOUP

Sprinkle the peanuts into a small skillet over medium-high heat. Cook, shaking the pan frequently, until the peanuts have darkened and become fragrant, just a few minutes. Immediately transfer them to a plate to cool; if you leave them to cool in the pan, they can burn.

Cut the Asian pear into large chunks; set aside a few of the chunks, then chop the rest finely and reserve for garnish. Stem and seed the jalapeño; if desired, reserve the seeds to add heat to the soup later. Cut the jalapeño into several pieces.

Combine the larger chunks of Asian pear with the jalapeño, mango, yogurt, garlic, lime juice, and ice cubes in a blender or the bowl of a food processor; puree until smooth. Taste and season with salt as needed. If desired, add the reserved jalapeño seeds a couple at a time, blending and tasting after each addition. Pour into a bowl. (If the soup seems too fibrous, push it through a fine-mesh strainer and into the bowl.)

Top with the tofu, peanuts, reserved chopped Asian pear, and cilantro, and eat.

2 tablespoons unsalted, raw peanuts

1/2 small Asian pear

1/2 Jalapeño

Flesh of 1 medium mango, cut into chunks (about 3/4 cup)

3/4 cup plain whole-milk yogurt

1 clove garlic

2 tablespoons freshly squeezed lime juice (from 1 lime)

2 ice cubes

Sea salt

1/4 cup Marinated and Baked Tofu (page 170) or store-bought baked or extra-firm tofu, cut into 1/2-inch cubes

Leaves from 3 or 4 sprigs of cilantro, finely chopped

*The first time I had gumbo z'herbes, the famous Leah Chase herself spooned it out of a pot at an event in New Orleans in 2006. I wasn't alone in swooning. Gumbo is made in all sorts of ways and with all sorts of ingredients in Louisiana, but this particular variety, a traditional Lenten dish, uses as many greens as the cook can find (the idea being that the more varieties you put in, the better your luck in the coming year). As a Good Friday dinner, it was originally meatless, but Chase and plenty of other Louisiana cooks can't help but add the flavor of smoky ham hocks, sausages, or other meats. I use a little smoked paprika instead (or, sometimes, when I'm feeling particularly sacrilegious, a little tempeh), but for omnivores who aren't subject to Lenten restrictions, a slice or two of bacon, fried up before you make the roux, goes beautifully with the greens. If you haven't made the greens already, use 2 cups of fresh kale, collard greens, Swiss chard, beet greens or a combination (the more, the merrier), stripped from their stems, thoroughly washed and dried, cut into thin ribbons, and then cooked in the stock with the rest of the ingredients until very tender.*

# GREEN GUMBO

Pour the oil into a medium skillet set over medium heat. When it shimmers, whisk in the flour and cook for a few minutes, until the raw flour taste is gone but the roux is still light, not browned. Sprinkle in the paprika and red pepper flakes and stir in the garlic, shallot, celery, and green pepper. Cook, stirring frequently, until the vegetables start to get tender. Add the greens and the liquid or stock mixture and cook another few minutes, just until the greens are hot and the flavors have melded.

Spoon the gumbo into a bowl over the rice, and eat.

1 tablespoon vegetable oil

1 tablespoon flour

1 teaspoon Spanish smoked paprika (pimentón)

1/4 teaspoon crushed red pepper flakes, or more to taste

2 cloves garlic, chopped

1 large shallot, chopped

1 celery heart, or 1/2 whole celery stalk, chopped

1/2 green pepper, stemmed, seeded, and chopped

1/2 cup cooked greens (page 173), lightly drained and chopped

3/4 cup greens cooking liquid, vegetable stock (opposite), water, or a combination

1 cup hot cooked brown (page 177) or white rice

# Vegetable Stock

I don't usually buy vegetable stock, because it's so easy to make at home. And I don't even shop for the ingredients to make it. Instead, I save up vegetable and herb trimmings, and when I have enough, I throw them into a stockpot with some garlic, water, and maybe a bay leaf and a few peppercorns and simmer away.

You can use all sorts of trimmings, but for the most neutral stock I prefer the peels and end trimmings of squash, asparagus, carrots, celery, onions, leeks, and garlic; stalks from Swiss chard (as much as I usually love kale, it can be too strongly flavored for stock); and stems from mushrooms, parsley, thyme, and rosemary. Rinse them if necessary, to avoid having to strain out any grit.

How much do you use? Put the trimmings as you have them into quart-sized freezer bags, storing them in the freezer as you go so you don't have to worry that they will spoil. Once you have two bags stuffed pretty full, transfer the contents to a big stockpot. Fill it with about 3 quarts of water, add 2 teaspoons of peppercorns and a couple of bay leaves, and bring to a boil. Reduce the heat until the liquid is at a bare simmer, cover the pot, and simmer until the vegetables are very tender and have lost their flavor (which has gone into the water), about 30 minutes. Strain out the solids, add salt to taste (if desired—you can also season it when you use it later), and let the stock cool; you should have about 2 quarts.

If you've got immediate plans for it, store the stock in an airtight container in the refrigerator for up to 1 week. But my favorite way to store is to freeze it in ice cube trays, then transfer the cubes to freezer bags and freeze for up to 6 months, pulling out as many—or as few—cubes as you need.

*The addition of avocado makes this cold soup creamier than your average gazpacho, and the greens make it, well, greener, and with jalapeño included, too, it's got a serious kick that makes it anything but traditional. It probably goes without saying, but if you serve this to Spaniards, either don't call it gazpacho or be prepared for some arguments at the table.*

# CREAMY GREEN GAZPACHO

Reserve one-quarter of the tomato, two cucumber chunks, two avocado chunks, and one basil leaf. Combine and finely chop for garnish.

Stem and seed the jalapeño half and reserve the seeds. Cut the jalapeño into several pieces. Combine one or two pieces of the jalapeño with the remaining tomato, cucumber, avocado, and basil and the watercress or spinach, celery, garlic, red wine vinegar, honey, and ice cubes in a blender or the bowl of a food processor; puree until smooth. Add $1/4$ cup or more water to thin the mixture, if necessary.

Taste and season with salt, pepper, and more vinegar, if needed. If you want the soup spicier, add more of the jalapeño, a little at a time, as well as some of the seeds if desired, blending and tasting after each addition. Refrigerate until cold, then pour into a bowl and top with the reserved chopped tomato, cucumber, avocado, and basil and a drizzle of olive oil, and eat.

1 medium tomato, cored and cut into quarters

1 small cucumber, peeled and cut into large chunks

Flesh from $1/2$ avocado, cut into large chunks

3 large basil leaves

$1/2$ jalapeño (optional)

$3/4$ cup lightly packed watercress or baby spinach leaves

1 small celery stalk (optional)

1 clove garlic, crushed

1 tablespoon red wine vinegar, or more to taste

1 tablespoon honey

2 ice cubes

Filtered water (optional)

Kosher or sea salt

Freshly ground black pepper

1 teaspoon extra-virgin olive oil

*I've said it for years: God help the single cook who is looking for a manageable amount of celery. Supermarkets sell it by the bunch, and most recipes—even those for a family—usually call for a stalk or two at the most. Herewith, a delicious way to use the rest of the bunch. Tart apples and blue cheese add pep to the sometimes bland celery. And because of the larger problem of all that celery, I recommend making this soup in larger quantities. Transfer the extra portions (without the garnishes of extra apple and blue cheese) to single-serving ziplock bags (see "A Vacuum Shortcut," page 171) and freeze for up to several months. Defrost in the refrigerator and add fresh garnishes when you are ready to eat it.*

# CELERY SOUP with APPLE and BLUE CHEESE

## MAKES ABOUT 5 CUPS, OR FOUR 1¼-CUP SERVINGS

Use a vegetable peeler to remove the outer stringy layer from the celery, and discard (or reserve for vegetable stock, page 59). Combine the stalks and any leaves, the shallots, stock, one of the apples, and ¼ cup of the blue cheese in a soup pot over medium-high heat, stirring to submerge the solids as much as possible; bring to a boil, then reduce the heat to medium or medium-low so the liquid is gently bubbling. Cover and cook until the celery and apples are tender, 20 to 25 minutes.

Use a hand-held immersion blender to puree until smooth, or transfer to a blender or food processor and carefully puree, working in batches if necessary. If you want to eat it cold, cool to room temperature, then transfer to an airtight container. Refrigerate until well chilled.

Stir in the yogurt. Season with salt and pepper to taste. Divide among individual bowls (or store the remaining soup as described in the headnote). Top each portion with the remaining chopped apple and a tablespoon of the blue cheese, and serve.

1 bunch (about 1½ pounds) celery with leaves

2 large shallot lobes, chopped

4 cups vegetable stock (page 59)

2 Granny Smith apples, peeled, cored, and finely chopped

½ cup crumbled blue cheese

½ cup plain whole-milk Greek-style yogurt (may substitute low-fat)

Kosher or sea salt

Freshly ground black pepper

*I don't know why it took me so long to realize that I could do something with poblano peppers other than roast them. Maybe it's because that's how so many recipes call for them to be used, but of course you can treat them as you would a bell pepper, which is what I do here, chopping and sautéing a poblano along with garlic and onions to form a powerful base for a hearty bean soup. The croutons may sound a little adventurous, but trust me, cinnamon plays very well here, offering a deep, somewhat mysterious flavor. Poblanos have a mild heat, so if you want to nudge this up a bit, feel free to add a little cayenne for that back-of-the-throat warmth. Omnivores, this practically cries out for a little bacon. Throw it in with the shallots, garlic, and poblano.*

# BEAN AND POBLANO SOUP with CINNAMON CROUTONS

Pour 1 tablespoon of the oil into a medium saucepan over medium heat. When it shimmers, add the bread pieces and fry until crisp and golden, about 2 minutes per side. Transfer to a paper towel–lined plate and immediately sprinkle with salt and about 1/4 teaspoon of the cinnamon.

Return the saucepan to medium heat, pour in the remaining 1 tablespoon of oil, and when it shimmers add the shallot, garlic, and poblano and cook, stirring occasionally, until the vegetables are tender. Sprinkle in the remaining 1/4 teaspoon of cinnamon and the cayenne, let the spices sizzle and bloom for a few seconds, then add the beans and 1/2 cup of the bean broth.

Bring the soup to a boil, then turn it down until it is barely simmering and cook until it thickens slightly, the flavors come together, and the beans, if they were cold, are heated through. Thin with the remaining 1/4 cup of bean broth if you'd like the soup to be a little thinner. Stir in the lime juice, then taste the soup and add salt and black pepper as needed, plus more cayenne pepper if you want more heat.

Spoon the soup into a bowl, top with the yogurt and the croutons, and eat.

- 2 tablespoons extra-virgin olive oil
- 1 slice rustic bread, cut or torn into bite-size pieces
- Sea salt
- 1/2 teaspoon cinnamon
- 1 large shallot lobe or very small onion, finely chopped
- 2 cloves garlic, finely chopped
- 1 poblano chile, stemmed, seeded, and finely chopped
- Pinch of cayenne pepper (optional), or more
- 1/2 cup cooked beans, preferably homemade (page 175), rinsed if canned, drained
- 1/2 to 3/4 cup bean broth, water, or vegetable stock (page 59)
- 1 tablespoon freshly squeezed lime juice (from 1/2 lime), or more to taste
- Freshly ground black pepper
- A dollop of yogurt or sour cream (optional)

*When I'm sick, I always crave two things: ginger and soup. But there's no reason to choose when you can add the throat-tingling heat of ginger to an earthy carrot soup. I like to brighten things up a little by tossing in some sweet-and-sour beet cubes. Even though I usually eat this one hot, you can chill it and eat it cold instead; the choice depends on the weather outside and your own need for body temperature adjustment.*

# CARROT and GINGER SOUP with QUICK-PICKLED BEET

Bring the vegetable stock to a boil in a small saucepan over medium-high heat. Add the beet, reduce the heat to medium-low so the stock is simmering, and cover. Cook until the beet is fork-tender, about 20 to 30 minutes. Remove the beet and let it cool. Transfer the stock, which will be colored pink from the beet, into a bowl and reserve to use in the soup. (If there are any stray pieces of beet peel in the stock, strain it.)

Pour 2 teaspoons of the olive oil into the saucepan over medium heat. When the oil shimmers, add the shallot and ginger and cook, stirring occasionally, until the shallot starts to soften. Stir in the carrots and strained broth; bring to a boil, then reduce the heat to medium-low so that the liquid is simmering, cover, and cook until the carrots are very tender, about 15 minutes.

Meanwhile, and when the beet is cool enough to handle, slip off its skin and cut it into 1/2-inch cubes. Toss in a small bowl with the rice vinegar, honey, and the remaining teaspoon of olive oil.

Use an immersion blender to puree the carrot mixture into a smooth soup, add salt to taste, and keep it warm until ready to eat. Alternatively, transfer to a blender and puree, removing the center knob in the blender's lid and holding a dish towel over it to avoid splattering, and return it to the saucepan to warm. Add water to the soup if desired.

Ladle the soup into a serving bowl, top with the beets and their liquid, and eat.

1 1/2 cups vegetable stock (page 59)

1 small beet, scrubbed but not peeled

1 tablespoon extra-virgin olive oil

1 large shallot, chopped

1 (1-inch) piece fresh ginger, peeled and grated

2 medium carrots, scrubbed and cut into 1/4-inch pieces

1 teaspoon rice vinegar, preferably unseasoned

1 teaspoon honey

Sea salt

*I could tell you how much I love Israeli couscous, those pearls of pasta that are so much more substantial than the fluffier variety. I could tell you how brilliant they are in this twist on the classic Italian pasta e fagioli. But what I should just admit is that this soup, as grown-up as it may seem, ends up tasting like the best-ever version of children's alphabet soup—and looking like it, too, if the alphabet consisted of all the dots over the "i"s and no actual complete letters. I first made it on a day when the sky cracked open and rain washed away my just-planted carrot seeds. I felt a childlike pout coming on, so I mothered myself, and all was right with the world. The carrots would be replanted another day.*

# BEAN and ISRAELI COUSCOUS SOUP

Strip the Swiss chard leaves from their stems. Finely chop the leaves and thinly slice the stems, keeping them separate.

Pour the oil into a medium saucepan set over medium heat. When the oil starts to shimmer, add the chard stems, onion, garlic, and anchovy and cook until the vegetables are tender, 3 or 4 minutes. Add the tomatoes, beans, and water, increase the heat to medium-high, and bring to a boil.

Stir in the couscous and chopped Swiss chard leaves and reduce the heat so the soup is at a simmer, then cover and cook until the couscous is tender and the soup has thickened, about 10 minutes. Add a little more water if needed to thin the soup out. Stir in the basil and cheese, then taste and add salt and pepper as needed. Eat hot.

4 large Swiss chard leaves

1 tablespoon extra-virgin olive oil

1 very small onion or large shallot, finely chopped

1 clove garlic, thinly sliced

1 anchovy fillet, finely chopped (optional)

3/4 cup crushed canned tomatoes

3/4 cup cooked pinto, cannellini, or other beans, preferably homemade (page 175), rinsed if canned, drained

1 cup water, vegetable stock, or liquid from homemade beans, plus more if needed

1/3 cup Israeli couscous

3 large basil leaves, stacked, rolled, and thinly sliced

2 tablespoons grated Parmigiano-Reggiano

Kosher or sea salt

Freshly ground black pepper

# SHOULD WE STOP MOCKING MOCK MEAT?

Let's face it—no one orders a T-bone steak because of its Sherman units and amino acids, but because it is thick and juicy and appetitive. Soup, cheese, apple strudel, and such things we eat because we like them. But vegetables? "Let's see—cabbage has Vitamin C; eggplant has G. I might manage a carrot or two, just for the A and the calcium." That's no spirit in which to eat.

**—IRMA G. MAZZA,** *Accent on Seasoning,* 1957

In Boston sometime in the early 1990s, my friends Lauren and Jamie wanted to take me to a place in Brookline that had a mission in triplicate: it was Chinese *and* kosher *and* vegan. Lauren had recently converted to vegetarianism because of Jamie, and this was one of their new hangouts. I was intrigued, but as I perused the menu of various noodle dishes, it was hard to ignore the fact that the most ubiquitous punctuation, by far, was the quotation mark. As in "Chicken" Lo Mein. This wasn't one of those misuses of the quotation mark for emphasis (as in All Our Pasta is "Hand Made") that drive me and copy editors the world over crazy. This chicken was properly qualified. It was "chicken" with a wink and a nudge. In other words, it wasn't chicken at all.

I wasn't interested in a gimmick, so I zeroed in on the quotation mark–free dishes, like Vegetable Fried Rice featuring good old vegetables that needed no qualification. And after I tasted the "chicken" Lauren ordered, I knew I'd made the right choice. (I did love the place's name, though, a play on its Hebrew connections: Shang Chai Delight, with the

"ch" pronounced with that clearing-the-throat feeling.)

But I made a mistake back then. Not in avoiding the stuff—I tried it and, to borrow a phrase, I just wasn't that into it. The mistake was in assuming that these products were some newfangled concoction dreamed up by people more interested in marketing or nutrition than in good food, or that perhaps they were a holdout of the hippie era, like Birkenstocks with socks. On the contrary, imitation meat—or what some of its makers today would rather call vegetarian meat (an oxymoron I can't quite get past)—is a tradition far older than Woodstock. It just didn't start in the West. If it had, perhaps that verse in Genesis that carnivores sometimes quote would read, "And God said, Let us make man in our image, after our likeness: and let them have dominion over the fish of the sea, and over the fowl of the air, and over the cattle, and over all the earth, and over every creeping thing that creeps upon the earth. And if they tire of such dominion, or decide it's not a good idea after reading *Forks Over Knives*, then let them take plants from the ground, and make them in the image and flavor of the fish of the sea, the fowl of the air, and of the cattle and of every creeping thing that creeps upon the earth. Let them call these creations Shamburgers and Tofurky. And let them charge good money for them in the temple that shall be called Whole Foods."

No, the tradition goes back to seventh-century China, where Buddhist monks and nuns discovered that by rinsing and kneading wheat flour, they would be left with a high-protein product malleable enough to play the part of meat; they called it *mien ching*. Over the following centuries, particularly in the temple cuisine of such cities as Hangzhou, cooks who were interested in putting the "art" into artifice starting shaping and cooking bean curd, wheat gluten, and mashed taro to make them look—and sometimes taste— like poultry, meat, or fish. "Efforts to duplicate meat flavors were often made, but it was more important for the artistic creation to look like food that was forbidden," writes Eileen Yin-Fei Lo in *Mastering the Art of Chinese Cooking.* "The intention was to fool the eye and thus surprise the palate." While soybean curd featured in some of that Buddhist cooking, my friend Andrea Nguyen points out in her book *Asian Tofu* that tofu itself wasn't developed to be a meat substitute; it is a beautiful, artisanal food enjoyed on its own terms—and often cooked and/or served with meat.

It wasn't until the middle of the twentieth century that soy, wheat gluten, and the like started to make their way west on the wings of the macrobiotic movement, which has ties to Japan and was picked up in the 1960s and 1970s by California hippies. And these days,

all it takes is a stroll through Whole Foods or most any other supermarket to see that imitation meat of all stripes is big business; more than a quarter of Americans, in fact, report using vegetarian meats at home. And as much as I disliked that Shang Chai "chicken," I've come around to some other mock meats in recent years, as the available flavors and textures have gotten better and the ingredient list simpler. The latter has been a relief, because I've long had some nagging little questions about the stuff. Namely, shouldn't vegetarians just eat vegetables, and get their protein from beans and nuts rather than eating processed food? For those who follow the "eat real food" mantra of writer Michael Pollan, avoiding ingredients their grandmother wouldn't recognize, there might be little room for the soy protein isolate and xanthan gum in something like the "Tuscan Breasts" made by Gardein.

But all vegetarian meats are not created equal. Coincidentally or not, some of the brands whose products I've found the most palatable say that the products are on the less processed side, with ingredients that my grandma might not recognize but that a Japanese *obaasan* might. Field Roast, the "grain meat" company David Lee started in Seattle in 1997, starts most of its products' ingredient lists with "vital wheat gluten" (the building block of Japanese seitan), which is similar to the *mien ching* those Buddhists were making so long ago. In the Japanese tradition, gluten and water are made into a paste and then simmered in broth; by contrast, Field Roast grinds the mixture with oil, vegetables, and spices to make, for example, its smoked apple-sage-grain meat sausage.

Lee, fifty-four, has perhaps as long a history with seitan as any American. When he lived in Boston in the 1970s, macrobiotic guru Michio Kushi introduced him to the food. Later, while helping develop a vegan teriyaki wrap for Essential Foods in Seattle, and in search of a filling firmer than tofu, he started making his own seitan. "I saw all these fake highly processed meats, and I wanted to make something that had handmade energy in it," he said. Particularly, he wanted to take the *mien ching* tradition and "marry it to the tradition of European charcuterie," adding the "big bold flavors" of the latter. Field Roast was born.

The company has had steady annual growth of 20 to 30 percent over the years, Lee says, but in 2012 that number hit 50 percent. Why the jump? "It's a number of things, one being that we've been around longer," he says, "but more importantly, there's a major shift happening. In the time I've been doing this, I've seen vegetarian and vegan become more and more accepted and mainstream." With people like Bill Clinton, Oprah Winfrey, Paul McCartney, and Ellen DeGeneres associated with veganism, how could it not?

Like Field Roast, Upton's Naturals emphasizes the culinary history behind its main ingredient, but it also puts the word "seitan" right in the names of its products, which include traditional ground beef–style, chorizo-style, and Italian sausage–style seitan. Actually, strike that. When I called company founder Daniel Staackmaan in his Chicago office, he told me that the company has been phasing in new packaging that eliminates "beef" and "sausage" from the product names. "We're distancing ourselves from any words that connect us to meat," he said.

About seven years ago, the thirty five-year-old Staackmann noticed that there was just one national manufacturer, and nobody was doing anything local. "People say, 'It's fake sausage,' but, well, not really," he told me. "Seitan is its own thing, and it's been around for hundreds and hundreds of years. We took that basic formula and seasoned it to taste like things that might be familiar to Americans who are trying to phase out meat."

Ah, I thought. He said it: "familiar." I heard the word, or a version of it, in several of my conversations with the makers of these products. And perhaps that's really the key to understanding the question of whether vegetarians ought to be focusing on eating vegetables, grains, and legumes. It's a question that others have asked, including *New York Times* columnist Mark Bittman. In a polite rebuttal to some of the issues Bittman raised about processed meat substitutes in a TED Talk, *Veganist* author Kathy Freston said the issue isn't really about whole foods versus fake meats; it's about getting more Americans to take baby steps. "When I led Oprah and her Harpo staffers through a 7-day vegan challenge recently, my approach was to take their current lifestyle and eating habits into account, and ease them into eating vegan by showing how easy it is to swap out fattening, high-cholesterol animal products for vegan versions of their traditional favorite foods," Freston wrote on the Huffington Post.

Lee would agree. Our food culture is so meat-centered, it's impossible to escape the meat references as a company like his tries to offer an alternative. "For a sandwich, what do you do? You get two pieces of bread and put some protein in there. So we're trying to provide something that we can hold onto culturally and that's satisfying. My mission is to make something that makes it easy for people not to eat animals."

Lee says Field Roast is the only vegetarian-meat company that uses fresh vegetables in its recipes. Staackmann says Upton's differentiates itself by adding no oil. And both of them knock the companies that more highly process their products, because that seems to them to go against the ethos of veganism, with its emphasis on the natural. Staackmann knows firsthand how, for a new vegan, the temptation of convenience products can sometimes trump common sense. He remembers being twenty or twenty-one and discovering donuts in a work vending machine that were "accidentally vegan," as he calls it. "I was so excited they were vegan that it didn't bother me that they had 44 grams of fat in each donut, and were loaded with hydrogenated fat," he said. "I ate two or three a day, and eventually it caught up with me."

Another high-profile product coming down the pike takes things in another direction entirely. Beyond Meat has gotten headlines for the fact that its early financial backers include two of Twitter's cofounders, Biz Stone and Evan Williams, and for blind taste tests that fooled Bittman, among others, into believing the company's product (called "chicken-free strips") was white-meat chicken. As of this writing, it was primarily available in Whole Foods stores in some regions, as an ingredient in wraps, veggie chicken salads, and other prepared foods.

As anyone who looks at photos on the company's website can tell, the product's most startling feature is its visual similarity to strips of chicken breast meat, down to the long fibers that tear like chicken. The similarity continues when you touch and taste it; it's uncanny, actually. But when I served it plain—and without explanation—to guests at a dinner party, the reaction was mixed. "This tastes starchy somehow," said one man, a local cheese maker. "Did you poach it in noodles?" Another said, "It tastes almost like the meat eater's version of tofu."

The next day, though, I dressed some in mayonnaise and basil-infused salt and thought it was pretty great. I knew it wasn't chicken, but that fact was difficult to keep in mind as I ate it. The texture was spot on.

Company founder Ethan Brown, who has a background in the clean energy industry, turned his attention to "meat analogs" when he realized that the environmental impact of industrial meat production is too profound to ignore. In a phone conversation, he rattled off some of the statistics, including the facts that 51 percent of the emissions that scientists believe are connected to climate change come from livestock and that chickens and pigs eat from 33 to 50 percent of the world's entire catch from the sea, by weight. "That's six times what the American consumer eats in seafood, and twice the Japanese," he said. "It's a massive vacuum of resources."

Brown spent ten years working with University of Missouri researchers to come up with the process and ingredient combination that would most effectively imitate the taste and texture of meat, then spent three years tweaking the product with his own team. Should something that high-tech really be part of the answer to industrial meat, environmentally speaking? Beyond Meat's website describes the product as "climate friendly and resource efficient," but I asked if this means it is more resource-efficient than, say, growing fruits and vegetables? No, he conceded. "The whole soybean or the whole pea would be more efficient, but you'd have to eat much more of it, and how long would it last? It's definitely not as efficient. But it's so much more efficient than meat."

The ingredient list is also not quite as benign-sounding as those of Field Roast and Upton's products (a few ingredients end in –ate and –ide), but that's something Brown wants to change. Perhaps the savviest thing about Brown's approach is his commitment to selling Beyond Meat at a competitive price. "Right now we're competitive with the natural chicken market, the antibiotic-free chicken," he says. "But as we scale and get into millions of pounds of capacity, we think we can drop below the price of boneless skinless chicken breasts at the high end. Our main focus is high-quality protein that's plant-based and underpriced."

Eventually, Brown hopes, vegetable- and animal-derived meat will be widely considered to be roughly equivalent, just as in the dairy aisle, where milk is no longer the exclusive product of cows and we can also choose among rice milk, soy milk, almond milk, and more.

Some of the press surrounding Beyond Meat has included statements from vegans that the product is frankly a little freaky to eat, that it seems so much like chicken it must be a trick. I didn't have any longtime vegetarians or vegans on my tasting panel, but when I mentioned the product to my friend Allen, he immediately said, "Why would I want to eat something that reminds me of meat? I don't like meat." Then he paused, "Well, I do sometimes like a veggie burger, but that's just so I have an excuse to put a lot of ketchup on a bun. I suppose I could just put a lot of ketchup on a bun, but that just seems wrong."

This conversation happened after I had made Allen the following for dinner: a simple salad of sliced and salted cherry tomatoes, cucumbers, and onion, showered in olive oil and punctuated with a little goat cheese; and a mushroom, broccoli, and caramelized onion puff pastry tart. No imitation meat in sight. But the next day, looking for a quick lunch to combine on bread with that tomato salad, I pulled out some Gardein BBQ Skewers I had bought out of curiosity the previous day. I pan-fried them in a little oil and tasted them. A little musty, a little weird. So I thought of Allen, reached for the ketchup, and started thinking about what honest-to-goodness vegetables—recognizable as the plants they are—I'd cook up for dinner that night.

## Chapter 3

# BAKING, ROASTING, and BROILING

Sometimes turning on the oven is the last thing you want to do, isn't it? Maybe it goes back to that it's-too-much-trouble-for-just-me feeling. If so, I want to help you get over it by reminding you that your oven can give you results with vegetables that can't be accomplished any other way. I'm especially enamored of high-heat roasting, whose effect on cauliflower, for one—creating caramelized edges and creamy interior—makes skeptics into believers. But I might be even fonder of the one oven technique that most approximates what happens on a grill: broiling. Start something on the stovetop, or at a lower temperature in the oven, then flash it under a super-hot broiler—crisping the edges of a sweet potato galette or getting a pomegranate glaze bubbling on eggplant—and you'll see what I mean.

The best part of a broiler might be that it gets going so quickly; little if any time is wasted waiting for it to preheat. But maybe your objection to the oven is that you find it wasteful to use all that energy for a single-serving meal. In that case, the remedy is at hand. While the oven is heating, prep whatever other vegetables you have in your pantry or fridge, and roast them alongside the dinner you're making. The next night, you'll find those already roasted potatoes, beets, peppers, or carrots and feel several steps ahead of the game.

*Who says eggplant parm (or, as they say in Boston, "pahm") has to either be made in a big casserole dish for a large Italian family or not at all? I got the idea from Mario Batali to deconstruct the thing into little stacks, which makes it eminently downscalable. Depending on the size of your eggplant and your appetite, this makes a single-serving meal with no accompaniments, or it can feed two with a salad and bread or another side dish.*

# BABY EGGPLANT PARM

## MAKES 1 OR 2 SERVINGS

Preheat the oven to 450°F. Line a rimmed baking sheet with aluminum foil.

Brush both sides of the eggplant slices with the oil, then lightly season the slices with salt and pepper on both sides. Roast until the eggplant starts to brown, 12 to 15 minutes, then transfer the eggplant slices to a plate.

Reduce the oven temperature to 350°F. Place the two largest roasted eggplant slices back on the baking sheet, then top each one with a large spoonful of the tomato sauce, sprinkles of basil and mozzarella, and a dusting of the Parmigiano-Reggiano. Top each with a second slice of roasted eggplant and repeat until you use all the cheese, the tomato sauce, and the eggplant; end with an eggplant slice if possible. Sprinkle with the bread crumbs, then drizzle lightly with oil.

Bake until the cheese has melted and is lightly browned, about 15 minutes, and eat.

1 small Japanese or baby Italian eggplant (8 to 10 ounces), unpeeled, cut into $3/4$-inch slices

2 teaspoons extra-virgin olive oil, plus more for drizzling

Sea salt

Freshly ground black pepper

$3/4$ cup Tomato Sauce with a Kick (page 176) or store-bought sauce

6 large basil leaves, stacked, rolled and cut crosswise into thin slices

$1/4$ cup grated mozzarella cheese

2 teaspoons freshly grated Parmigiano-Reggiano

2 teaspoons plain dried bread crumbs

*In the South, whenever there's a funeral, there's food like spinach rice casserole, baked up so fabulously gooey that you might forget that there's spinach in there. And I suppose that's the point. But if you like your greens, you might want to treat them in a way that showcases their flavor a bit more. I combine the rice with tomatoes, za'atar, and pistachio nuts, then layer the greens and cheese on top for a quick trip under the broiler. There's no need to bake a casserole when it's dinner for one and not a funeral buffet. Za'atar, for the uninitiated, is a blend of sumac, thyme, sesame seeds, and sometimes other herbs; it's available at good spice stores such as Penzeys or you can make your own (page 169). Note: If you don't have cooked greens already in your fridge, you can add 2 cups chopped leaves of kale, collards, or chard right after the za'atar and cook until the greens are wilted, then add the tomatoes and cook the whole combination together rather than layering it.*

# CHEESY GREENS and RICE GRATIN

Preheat the oven broiler, and adjust the rack to be several inches from the flame.

Pour the olive oil into a small cast-iron or other ovenproof skillet over medium heat. When it shimmers, add the garlic and cook until it starts to become tender. Sprinkle in the za'atar and cook for just a few seconds, letting the spices bubble and bloom. Stir in the tomatoes or sauce and rice, taste, and add salt as needed. Cook for a few minutes to let the flavors combine, then turn off the heat. Stir in the pistachios.

Pack the rice mixture down evenly with a spatula and top with the greens, leaving a ring of rice exposed. Sprinkle with the cheese. Slide the skillet under the broiler and cook until the cheese is melted, bubbly, and slightly browned, 3 or 4 minutes, then remove. Let cool slightly, but eat it hot.

1 tablespoon extra-virgin olive oil

2 cloves garlic, thinly sliced

1 teaspoon Za'atar (page 169)

1/4 cup canned crushed tomatoes in their liquid, or 2 chopped plum tomatoes, or 1/4 cup Tomato Sauce with a Kick (page 176)

3/4 cup cooked brown rice (page 177)

Sea salt

2 tablespoons roasted shelled pistachios, chopped

3/4 cup cooked greens (page 173), drained and squeezed of extra liquid

1/4 cup grated or chopped Taleggio, Gruyère, or other good melting cheese

## TIP

To store the remaining crushed tomatoes from the can, transfer the tomatoes and their juices to a glass jar and refrigerate for up to 1 week, or transfer to a ziplock bag and freeze for up to 6 months (see "A Vacuum Shortcut," page 171).

*When did it become so fashionable to eat just the thinnest of asparagus spears, barely steamed? Especially if they are farm-fresh, I prefer the fat, meatier spears, which give me more to sink my teeth into, and I like to char them slightly under the broiler. Asparagus—like plenty of other things—is delicious with the traditional Spanish romesco sauce, but the latter requires fresh tomatoes, which where I live aren't in season as early as asparagus. So I improvise, using put-up or store-bought salsa instead of tomatoes. Salsa verde (for which I have a killer recipe in Serve Yourself) turns the sauce a gorgeous cream color (hence the "blanco") and adds a hint of spice, while fresh mint keeps things, well, fresh. You may have slightly more sauce than you need, but it keeps for several days, covered, in the refrigerator. Thin it out with a little more vinegar and oil, and you've got an excellent salad dressing for another day.*

# ASPARAGUS with ROMESCO BLANCO

Sprinkle the almonds into a small skillet over medium-high heat. Cook, shaking the pan frequently, until the almonds have darkened and become fragrant, just a few minutes. Immediately transfer them to a plate to cool; if you leave them to cool in the pan, they can burn.

Set the oven to broil, and arrange a rack to be 5 or 6 inches from the flame. Snap the woody ends off the asparagus and discard them (or reserve them for vegetable stock), and toss the asparagus with 1 teaspoon of the olive oil on a rimmed baking sheet. Sprinkle with salt. Broil until the asparagus blackens in spots and the spears just barely bend when you lift them, about 5 to 10 minutes depending on the freshness and size of the asparagus. Remove from the oven.

While the asparagus is broiling, combine the salsa verde with the remaining 1 tablespoon of olive oil and the almonds, bread, mint, vinegar, and water in the bowl of a small food processor or blender, and puree until smooth, adding a little more water if the mixture seems too thick. Taste and add salt and vinegar as desired.

Eat the asparagus over the rice with about ¼ cup of the sauce spooned on top.

1 tablespoon sliced or slivered almonds

6 to 8 fat asparagus spears

1 tablespoon plus 1 teaspoon extra-virgin olive oil

Sea salt

2 tablespoons salsa verde, homemade or store-bought

½ small slice bread, preferably stale, torn into small pieces

2 large mint leaves

1 teaspoon apple cider vinegar, plus more as needed

2 teaspoons water, plus more as needed

½ cup warm cooked brown basmati rice (page 177) or another grain

*When I've got puff pastry in the freezer, all seems right with the world. Dinner is a half hour away, and if a spontaneous party were to break out in my apartment (a boy can dream, can't he?), I'd have the makings of cheese straws, or little mini-tarts, or who knows what else. The thing is, tarts like this take to all manner of seasonal combinations (see page 80). If you don't have caramelized onions already made and want to dive right into this recipe, you can thinly slice and sauté a small onion instead and use that as a base.*

# OYSTER MUSHROOM and CORN TART

Preheat the oven to 425°F. Line a small baking sheet with parchment paper.

On a lightly floured countertop, roll out the puff pastry slightly, to about 6 inches square. Pierce the dough every half-inch with a fork; this helps the pastry rise more evenly.

Transfer the dough to the prepared baking sheet. Gently spread the caramelized onions on the dough, leaving at least an inch all around the edges. Sprinkle with the corn kernels, then top with the mushrooms, a sprinkling of salt, and the thyme leaves. (It may seem like too much filling, but the mushrooms will shrink as they cook.) Pinch off small pieces of the goat cheese and dot them on the tart.

Lightly moisten the edges of the dough with water, and fold each edge over onto itself, forming a rim of pastry that overlaps the filling slightly. Use the tines of a fork to crimp the edges.

Bake the tart until the pastry has puffed and turned golden brown, 20 to 30 minutes. Transfer it to a plate and eat.

1 (5-by-5-inch) square frozen store-bought puff pastry, preferably all-butter (such as Dufour brand), defrosted but still cold

2 tablespoons Caramelized Onions (page 166), or 1 small sautéed onion

1/3 cup fresh corn kernels (see page 180) or thawed frozen corn

1/2 cup oyster mushrooms, cleaned and cut into 1/2-inch pieces (may substitute cremini, portobello, or stemmed shiitake mushrooms)

Sea salt

Leaves from 1 sprig of fresh thyme

1 tablespoon soft goat cheese

# More Savory Tart Ideas

As long as you have puff pastry in the freezer and Caramelized Onions (page 166) in the refrigerator, many possibilities for a quick dinner present themselves. Use the procedure described in Oyster Mushroom and Corn Tart (page 79) as a guide: put the onions on the bottom but, for the remaining toppings, substitute the following, which include some of my favorite combinations. Make sure to add salt to taste, and if the fillings look dry, feel free to add a little drizzle of olive oil.

**Tomato and Feta:** $1/2$ cup slow-roasted tomato halves, pinch Za'atar (page 169), $1/4$ cup crumbled feta

**Spring Pea and Lettuce:** $1/2$ cup shelled peas (fresh or thawed frozen), 1 cup chopped romaine lettuce, $1/4$ cup ricotta salata cheese, 2 tablespoons chopped mint leaves

**Potato and Rosemary:** 2 or 3 boiled and sliced small new potatoes, 1 tablespoon chopped fresh rosemary leaves, 2 tablespoons grated Pecorino Romano cheese

**Brussels Sprouts and Apple:** $3/4$ cup finely shredded brussels sprouts, 1 cored and sliced small tart apple, 1 tablespoon grated ginger

*Roasting is by far my favorite way to cook cauliflower, especially at high enough heat to get the florets browned and caramelized and crispy on the edges. When combined with green beans and drizzled with a tart-spicy chipotle sauce, the humble cauliflower becomes almost elegant. Double the portions and leave out the grain for a side dish that serves four.*

# ROASTED CAULIFLOWER and GREEN BEANS with CHIPOTLE SAUCE

Preheat the oven to 450°F.

On a rimmed baking sheet, toss the cauliflower and green beans with olive oil and sprinkle generously with salt. Roast until the vegetables are tender and the cauliflower is nicely browned on the edges, 20 to 30 minutes, tossing them once or twice during the cooking to keep things even.

While the vegetables are roasting, sprinkle the pecans into a small skillet over medium-high heat. Cook, shaking the pan frequently, until the nuts start to brown and become fragrant, a few minutes. Immediately transfer them to a plate to cool; if you leave them to cool in the pan, they can burn. Once they are cool, chop them.

In a small bowl, stir together the yogurt and adobo sauce. Taste and add more salt if desired.

Remove the cauliflower and green beans from the oven and let cool slightly before transferring to a serving bowl over the rice. Drizzle with the sauce, sprinkle with the cilantro and pecans, and eat.

- 1/4 medium cauliflower, cut into bite-size florets (about 1 cup)
- 1 cup green beans, trimmed

  Olive oil

  Sea salt
- 2 tablespoons raw unsalted pecans
- 1/3 cup plain whole-milk yogurt (may substitute low-fat or nonfat)
- 1 teaspoon adobo sauce from canned chipotles in adobo, or 1/2 teaspoon ground chipotle

  Leaves from 4 sprigs of cilantro, chopped
- 1/2 cup warm cooked brown basmati rice (page 177) or other grain

## TIP

To store the remaining contents of the canned chipotle in adobo, transfer it to a glass jar and refrigerate for up to 1 month, or freeze in a ziplock bag for up to 6 months (see "A Vacuum Shortcut," page 171).

*A confession: I've never had* socca *(the name for this pancake from Nice) in its birthplace. I've never had* farinata, *the Italian version, in Genoa, nor* cecina *in Tuscany, nor the Indian iteration,* chila, *on the streets of Mumbai. But I started making this pancake periodically for an easy dinner party appetizer, seasoned with lots of rosemary and salt and nothing else on top. And then I started thinking about it as a fantastic stand-in for pizza when I didn't have time to make dough. It's not the same, but the crispy-creamy texture and the beany taste have charms all their own. Here I top it with Ottoman Eggplant Dip (page 149) and steamed broccoli, but many other good topping possibilities abound: caramelized onion and olive, pureed squash and tomatoes, roasted eggplant slices, even hummus and fried chickpeas for a triple-garbanzo threat. Note that chickpea flour goes by a few other names, including gram flour or* besan *in Indian markets and garbanzo bean flour in natural foods stores.*

# CHICKPEA PANCAKE with BROCCOLI and EGGPLANT PUREE

Preheat the oven to 450°F.

Whisk together the chickpea flour, salt, water, and 1 tablespoon of the olive oil until smooth.

Put a small (preferably 8-inch) cast-iron skillet over medium heat, and when it's hot, pour in the remaining 1 tablespoon of olive oil. When the oil shimmers, pour in the chickpea batter and transfer the skillet to the oven.

Bake until the pancake is golden brown on top and pulls away from the edge of the pan, about 20 to 25 minutes. Remove the skillet from the oven, turn the oven to broil, and set an oven rack so the skillet will be 4 to 5 inches from the flame.

While the pancake is baking, put the broccoli pieces in a steamer basket over an inch of water in a small saucepan, set over medium heat, cover, and steam for a few minutes until the broccoli brightens and becomes crisp-tender.

When the pancake has finished baking, smear the eggplant dip on top, and lay the blanched broccoli slices on top. Grind on a generous amount of black pepper and sprinkle on the feta and Parmigiano-Reggiano. Slide the skillet under the broiler and broil until the cheese has melted and the broccoli has slightly browned, just a minute or two. Remove, let slightly cool, and slide onto a plate. Cut it into wedges and eat.

$1/2$ **cup chickpea flour**

$1/4$ **teaspoon salt, plus more to taste**

$1/2$ **cup water**

2 **tablespoons olive oil**

1 **very small head or several florets broccoli, sliced**

$1/4$ **cup Ottoman Eggplant Dip (page 149) or store-bought baba ghanoush**

**Freshly ground black pepper**

1 **tablespoon crumbled feta**

1 **tablespoon grated Parmigiano-Reggiano**

*It wasn't until I asked* Washington Post *readers to send me their favorite large-scale recipes to cut down to size, and I got a version of this, that I ever thought of making enchiladas—one of the favorite foods of my young adulthood—in a smaller portion. But if you've already got some sauce, it works like a charm. These are also excellent with a tomatillo salsa verde, either a store-bought version or the one I include in* Serve Yourself, *instead of the tomato sauce. Eat these with rice, beans, and/or a salad.*

# SPINACH ENCHILADAS

Preheat the oven to 350°F.

Pour the oil into a small skillet over medium heat. When it shimmers, add the shallot, garlic, and jalapeño and cook until soft but not browned. Add the spinach and stir-fry until it has just wilted, then scrape the mixture into a bowl and stir in the yogurt. Season with salt to taste.

Warm the tortillas to make them more pliable: either microwave them for a few seconds, or heat them in a dry skillet over medium-high heat for about 10 seconds on each side—not enough to brown them, just enough to soften them. (If you have a gas stove, you can also put them directly on the burner grate over the flame for a few seconds on each side.) Immediately wrap them in foil to keep them warm.

Pour the thinned-out tomato sauce into the skillet that you sautéed the shallot mixture in and bring it to a boil over medium heat, then reduce the heat to low so that the sauce is barely simmering. Use tongs to dip the tortillas into the sauce one at a time, leaving them in for just a few seconds; lift them out, letting the excess sauce drip off, and transfer them to a plate.

Spread about a quarter of the sauce on the bottom of a small casserole or individual gratin dish. Lay the softened tortillas on a work surface. Place half the spinach mixture in the center of each one, then roll the tortillas to form enchiladas and arrange them seam side down on top of the layer of sauce in the casserole dish. Spoon the remaining sauce on top and sprinkle with the grated cheese.

Bake until the cheese has melted and the sauce is bubbling, about 20 minutes. Sprinkle the enchiladas with the cilantro, and eat hot.

1 tablespoon olive oil

1 large shallot lobe, chopped

1 clove garlic, chopped

1/2 jalapeño, stemmed, seeded, and chopped

3 cups lightly packed baby spinach leaves, washed and dried

2 tablespoons whole Greek-style yogurt (may substitute low-fat or nonfat)

Sea salt

2 (6-inch) corn tortillas

2/3 cup Tomato Sauce with a Kick (page 176) or store-bought tomato sauce, thinned with 2 to 3 tablespoons of water

1/4 cup grated Monterey Jack cheese

1 tablespoon chopped cilantro leaves

*My love for the simple roasted sweet potato is everlasting. And when it comes to toppings, I don't know if it's the tropical connection or what, but sweet potatoes and coconuts are natural partners. I've become addicted to the use of coconut oil instead of butter on a roasted sweet potato—not because I want the dish to be vegan, but because I love the oil's nuttiness. From there, it was an easy decision one day to play up this nutty/sweet combo by reaching for shredded dried coconut (in two sizes for textural variation), walnuts, and dates.*

# ROASTED SWEET POTATO with COCONUT, DATES, and WALNUTS

Preheat the oven to 425°F.

Use a fork or sharp knife to prick the sweet potato in several places. Place on a piece of aluminum foil and bake until the potato is tender and can be easily squeezed, 30 to 40 minutes. (Alternatively, to speed up the process, the pricked sweet potato can be microwaved on high for 1 minute, then carefully transferred to a piece of foil and into the oven. Bake until the potato is tender, 20 to 30 minutes.)

While the potato is baking, sprinkle the walnuts into a small skillet over medium-high heat. Cook, shaking the pan frequently, until the nuts start to brown and become fragrant, a few minutes. Immediately transfer them to a plate to cool; if you leave them to cool in the pan, they can burn. Once they are cool, chop them.

Transfer the sweet potato to a serving plate. Use a knife to slash it open, then spoon the coconut oil on top, mashing it in. Sprinkle with salt to taste, then add the finely shredded coconut, walnuts, dates, and large coconut flakes, and eat.

1 small sweet potato (6 to 8 ounces)

3 tablespoons raw unsalted walnut halves

1 teaspoon virgin coconut oil (may substitute butter, olive oil, or walnut oil)

Kosher or sea salt

1 teaspoon finely shredded unsweetened coconut

2 or 3 pitted dates, preferably Medjool, chopped

1 tablespoon large unsweetened coconut flakes

# More Roasted Sweet Potato Ideas

When you keep a well-stocked pantry, you can turn the simplest roasted sweet potato into a satisfying meal. Here are some of my other favorite combinations. Follow the roasting instructions on page 90 and top with these ingredients in this order.

**Southwestern:** $1/2$ teaspoon ground cumin, $1/2$ teaspoon sea salt, $1/4$ cup cooked and drained black beans (page 175), chopped flesh of 1 grilled poblano chile (page 48), 2 tablespoons sour cream or Greek-style yogurt, 1 tablespoon freshly squeezed lime juice, and 2 tablespoons toasted pumpkin seeds

**Spanish:** $1/2$ teaspoon smoked Spanish paprika (pimentón), $1/2$ teaspoon sea salt, 1 tablespoon extra-virgin olive oil, $1/4$ cup chopped dried figs, 2 tablespoons toasted almonds (preferably Marcona), and 2 tablespoons grated Manchego cheese

**Southeast Asian:** $1/2$ teaspoon fish sauce, $1/2$ teaspoon chile-garlic paste or Thai red curry paste, and $1/2$ cup Marinated and Baked Tofu (page 170) or store-bought baked or extra-firm tofu, 1 tablespoon freshly squeezed lime juice, 2 tablespoons bean sprouts, 2 tablespoons roasted peanuts

**Japanese:** 1 teaspoon soy sauce, 1 tablespoon red or white miso paste, 2 teaspoons freshly grated ginger, $1/4$ cup chopped Grilled Cabbage (page 165) or thinly sliced raw Chinese cabbage, and 1 thinly sliced green onion

*When I want something a little fancier than a roasted sweet potato with toppings, I make this savory cake, built on the principles of the classic French potato galette (what Julia Child and company called galette de pommes de terre). Rather than make it a side dish, like the French, I stuff mine with hearty vegetables to make it a meal. This is a hearty portion, so if you're serving two, just add a crisp green salad topped with more vegetables, and split the galette. By the way, if the name threw you for a loop and you were expecting a rustic, free-form pastry, remember that galette is French for "cake," and the culinary term has been used for anything resembling one. If you have greens already cooked and on hand (page 173), you can use those instead of the raw kale; just combine about 1/3 cup of them with the mushrooms after cooking the latter.*

# SWEET POTATO GALETTE with MUSHROOMS and KALE

Preheat the oven to 400°F.

Strip the kale leaves from the stems and coarsely chop the leaves. Thinly slice the stems and keep them separate from the leaves.

Pour 1 tablespoon of the oil into a medium skillet over medium heat. When it starts to shimmer, sprinkle in the pimenton and let it sizzle and bloom for a few seconds, then add the onion, garlic, and sliced kale stems and sauté until tender. Add the mushrooms and sauté until they collapse and release their liquid, then add the kale leaves and continue cooking until the liquid has evaporated. Season with salt to taste and remove from the heat.

Pour the remaining tablespoon of oil into a small, well-seasoned cast-iron skillet over medium heat. Carefully arrange half of the sweet potato slices in the skillet in concentric circles, overlapping to form a couple of layers; sprinkle each layer with a little salt as you go. Spoon on the mushroom-kale mixture, and top with the grated cheese.

Arrange the remaining sweet potato slices on top, sprinkling each layer lightly with salt as you go. Press the galette with a spatula, cover the skillet tightly with aluminum foil, and bake until the sweet potatoes are easily pierced with a fork, 20 to 25 minutes.

| | |
|---|---|
| 1 | cup lightly packed kale leaves |
| 2 | tablespoons extra-virgin olive oil |
| 1/2 | teaspoon smoked Spanish paprika (pimentón), or 1/4 teaspoon crushed red pepper flakes (for more heat) |
| 1 | very small onion or large shallot lobe, finely chopped |
| 1 | clove garlic, thinly sliced |
| 4 | ounces oyster or other variety meaty mushrooms, stemmed and chopped |
| | Kosher or sea salt |
| 1 | small (6- to 8-ounce) sweet potato, scrubbed but not peeled, cut in 1/8-inch slices |
| 2 | tablespoons grated Comté, Gruyère, or other nutty mountain cheese |
| 2 | tablespoons raw unsalted pecan or walnut halves |
| 1 | green onion, trimmed and thinly sliced |

continued >

While the galette is baking, sprinkle the pecans into a small skillet over medium-high heat. Cook, shaking the pan frequently, until the nuts start to brown and become fragrant, a few minutes. Immediately transfer them to a plate to cool; if you leave them to cool in the pan, they can burn. Once they are cool, chop them.

Remove the galette from the oven and take off the foil. Turn the oven to broil and slide the skillet under the broiler element or flame until the sweet potatoes just brown on top.

Let the galette cool for a few minutes, then run a knife around the edges of the skillet to loosen it. Invert a plate over the skillet and, using oven mitts, hold the skillet and plate together and quickly flip the two so the plate is on the bottom and set it on the counter. Lift off the skillet. Some of the potato slices may stick to the pan; use a spatula to scrape them out and patch up the galette.

Sprinkle with the green onion slices and nuts and eat. (If you prefer, you can leave the galette in the pan and cut wedges out of it for eating.)

*Eggplant can take its time getting tender in the oven, but it's worth it, especially for preparations like this, where za'atar, with its earthy flavor, and sweet-tart pomegranate molasses turn things toward the Middle East. You can find both in Middle Eastern markets; za'atar can be had at good spice stores such as Penzeys, or you can make your own (page 169). Or substitute 1 teaspoon of dried thyme or oregano, a squeeze of lemon, and 1 teaspoon of sesame seeds.*

# POMEGRANATE-GLAZED EGGPLANT

Preheat the oven to 400°F.

Put a small, dry skillet over medium-low heat. Add the pine nuts and cook, shaking the pan and tossing the nuts frequently, until they are lightly browned and fragrant. Watch them carefully, and keep them moving, so they don't burn. Immediately transfer them to a plate to cool; if you leave them in the pan, even off the heat, they could burn.

Brush the cut side of the eggplant halves with oil and sprinkle them with za'atar and a little salt. Set the halves on a large piece of aluminum foil and fold it up to tightly enclose them. Put the foil packet on a small baking sheet and bake until the eggplant is fork tender, 30 to 40 minutes.

When the eggplant is tender, remove it from the oven, turn the oven to broil, and arrange a rack so the eggplant will be just a few inches from the flame. Open the foil packet, brush the eggplant with the pomegranate molasses, and broil just until the molasses is bubbly, about a minute.

Drizzle the juices from the foil packet over the rice. Top with the eggplant halves and scatter on the cherry tomatoes, mint, feta, and pine nuts.

1 tablespoon pine nuts

1 small (5- to 8-ounce) eggplant, halved lengthwise through the stem

2 teaspoons extra-virgin olive oil

2 teaspoons Za'atar (page 169)

Sea salt

2 teaspoons pomegranate molasses

1/2 cup warm cooked brown basmati rice (page 177) or another grain

6 large cherry tomatoes, quartered

4 large mint leaves, chopped

2 tablespoons crumbled feta

# Profile:
# THE FARMER GOES TO MARKET

Why do farmers farm, given their economic adversities on top of the many frustrations and difficulties normal to farming? And the answer is: love. They must do it for love.

—WENDELL BERRY, *Bringing it to the Table: Writings on Farming and Food*, 2009

Zach Lester is a blur. He's fetching bin after bin of kale, basil, green beans, potatoes, tomatoes—more things than I can count—from a refrigerated walk-in, stacking them on a roller, and sliding them across the barn to his box truck. It's not just that he's moving so quickly; it's that I'm moving so slowly, because it's 3 o'clock in the morning. Zach's destination—the Sunday farmers' market in the Dupont Circle neighborhood of Washington, DC—is a two-hour drive, and while it doesn't open for another 5¹/₂ hours, the farmer doesn't want to take any chances. "I like to be the first one there," he tells me as I drag myself up and into the passenger seat. In gracious understanding of my situation, he has packed me an all-important breakfast: a thermos full of coffee.

This is not a time of day with which I am familiar—or comfortable. But I want to see what it's like for a so-called truck farmer like Zach to pick, pack, drive, and sell some of the best produce I've ever tasted. These weekly trips are the backbone of his livelihood, as they are for so many like him. The number of farmers' markets all over the country has been growing at a rate of 10 percent or more every year, giving small farmers like Zach access to the kind of financial stability that would never come from the commodity prices and government subsidies that big agribusiness depends on. That means markets, CSAs (subscription programs), and other direct-to-consumer approaches may be the best hope for saving America's family farm. I've long done the bulk of my shopping at farmers' markets for just this reason, because I want to support local agriculture, but there's a selfish reason at work, too: I want delicious food, and farmers' markets represent my best chance of getting it.

The Dupont market is just a few minutes' walk from my apartment, and Zach became my favorite vendor soon after the first time I wandered into his stand six years ago, when I was struck by three things. First, the meticulously arranged stacks, which made sense once I heard he had been a landscape designer. Second, the quality of the vegetables as I started touching and smelling them, and the taste once I got to sample them. Third, by Zach himself and his smiling colleague, Katherine Stewart, both of whom always looked as healthy, bright, and ruddy as carrots, as if they, too, had been yanked up out of the ground by their hair and were still shaking off the rich soil.

Their farm, Tree and Leaf, wouldn't have scored coveted market spots if it hadn't been for the generosity of their landlords. In 2006, Zach and his wife, Georgia O'Neal, and Katherine started farming on land they leased from Wheatland Vegetable Farms in Purcellville, VA, where owners Chip and Susan Planck were scaling back their own production and helping cultivate a new generation of farmers. The Plancks persuaded the managers of the Dupont and Falls Church markets to let Tree and Leaf apply for the spots they were vacating. A few years later, in 2009, Zach and Georgia got a USDA mortgage to buy their own farm in Unionville, VA, almost two hours south. The move involved taking a winter-long break from the market scene while they got the new land plowed, planted, and harvested in time to start selling again in spring 2010.

With that behind them, this winter was difficult by all counts: Their leased truck broke down, forcing them to borrow a smaller one. Their second child, Addison, was born four and a half weeks early and spent eighteen days in the hospital. ("I was pulled out of the radish field and got there ten minutes before, covered in mud," Zach says. Addison is perfectly happy and healthy.) Then Katherine, their most prized farming partner, decided to leave, mostly to find a situation where she could work a little less and spend a little more

time finding her own spouse, Zach says. The loss of his friend—and the farm's manager—pains him, and every time he talks about it his brow furrows, he squints, and some of the brightness drains from his blue eyes.

Something else has changed about Zach since the last time I saw him: He's short-haired and clean-shaven, after decades of wearing a long braid and a beard, and has lost thirty pounds. He's downright tired on this day (most days, I imagine), but this ruddy carrot has been freshly scrubbed. "A clean start," he says. "A paradigm shift. Now that it's just me at the markets, I figured, if I'm going to be the face, it's going to be a clean face."

Zach is in a reflective mood; when I meet him at Falls Church, he has just come from a funeral for Dick Storch, a philanthropist and preservation-minded real estate developer who had leased him land in the historic village of Waterford, and who died at age 75 of lymphoma. Despite a nagging cough, Zach spends the drive back and forth to the city talking about Storch, and about his own successes and struggles big and small: the loss of $75,000 in tomato crops his first year in Unionville because of blistering summer heat; his love for Spa World, a huge Korean-run spa in Centreville, VA, where he goes every couple of weeks in the winter to "de-tune"; his philosophies of growing and selling; and his difficulty finding dependable workers, exacerbated by the loss of Katherine. Zach leans most heavily on Santiago, a Mexican man who has worked at Tree and Leaf for years. The two of them handle the bulk of the work tending the ten acres and huge greenhouses he has in production. A couple of interns are usually assisting at any given time, but even if they're hard-working, Zach says, they don't necessarily have the passion for farming he wants to see.

Now that Georgia is working less and less on the farm so she can care for their two boys, Zach finds himself needing to be three things in one: leader, manager, producer. As someone whose guiding principle is sustainability, he realizes this situation is anything but sustainable. "Leading is right-brain activity," he says, "and management is left-brain. I think about it like this: The leader looks over the jungle, the managers are sharpening the saws, and the producers are blazing the trail. Then the leader says, 'Oops! Wrong jungle!'"

Zach doesn't think he's plowing through the wrong jungle, so to speak, in Unionville, but he is mulling some shifts in direction. The night before heading to Dupont, Zach and I drive around the property just before dusk, and he talks about wanting to change the orientation of the vegetable beds on his main 18-acre field, half of it fallow because of rotation. They should be perpendicular to the 25 acres of woodland that border it, he thinks, to better take advantage of whatever permaculture might crawl from wood to field. He also wants to eventually manage and use the woods to heat the house, avoiding the need to buy heating oil. He's a devotee of four-season gardening, growing greens in high tunnels throughout the winter, and maybe the wood would help him heat one of the greenhouses. And those oaks! They'd be a prime spot to start cultivating shiitake mushrooms. It's obvious that no matter how tired he says he's getting, the man doesn't stop dreaming.

He pulls over so we can step out into the radish patch. It's early September, which means that the blistering summer heat is over and crops like radishes can come into play again. He crouches and pulls up a huge Luobo radish, a prized Chinese variety that are usually the size of baking potatoes; these are even bigger. "Look at that!" he exclaims. "What did I do right? I guess I know what will happen at the market tomorrow. I guess I'll be the radish man."

On the other side of the woods is his "magic patch," a rolling grassy field with clusters of trees. Eventually, if he's able to find a partner to manage the farm, he'd love to build the family house back here, and plant sour cherries, blueberries, currants, elderberries, all of which he calls "antioxidant fruits." Given the taste of the blueberries he grew on his previous land—they were the best I've tasted outside Maine—I'm an enthusiastic supporter of this idea.

It doesn't take long on this tour of his farm before I realize that since moving to DC in 2006, I've learned a lot of what I know about heirloom fruit and vegetable varieties from a handful of farmers, and Zach is one of them. When he talks about his love for Romanesco cauliflower, for instance—that green variety that looks like some mathematical fractal pattern, or possibly an alien planet—I start to say, "Absolutely, that's one of my favorites," then catch myself. Years ago, I bought my first head from Tree and Leaf. He laughs.

After helping one of the interns clean and bundle a variety of frilly purple basil in preparation for the next day's market, Georgia is in the house tending to Addison and thinking about plans for dinner. Their older son, six-year-old Eoin, is spending the night with friends, and Zach is angling for a little break from all this talking, and wants "fifteen minutes of me time" before eating. So I help Georgia with the cooking: Like me, they're mostly vegetarian, but she's roasting a small whole trout they got from the same farmers who supply their raw milk, and is pan-roasting some of their own fingerling potatoes, a buttery French variety called La Ratte. She has smashed the latter between two skillets, getting a nice sear before turning down the heat and letting them slowly sizzle and hiss on the way to tenderness. And she tasks me with shredding some watermelon radishes—so called because a slice of them reveals a red, white, and green pattern that looks like a cartoon version of the fruit—for a simple salad tossed with sesame oil, rice vinegar, ginger, and a splash of Bragg's amino acids. All of it is right up my alley, which isn't a surprise given that I've been talking to Zach and Katherine for years about the best ways to cook their produce.

To drink? Milk or water. Zach doesn't crack open a beer or pop the cork on a bottle of wine, another change from his longstanding habit, especially as a player of Irish music used to hanging out in bars. He stopped drinking the previous year, not because he thought he was alcoholic, but simply because he prefers how he feels—less "fuzzy," he says—without it. I'm relieved, because as much as I like a glass of wine with dinner, tomorrow is going to start early enough, and the last thing I need is even a hint of a hangover.

As predicted, we're the first to arrive at the Dupont market, pulling into the parking lot behind the PNC Bank in Dupont Circle in the morning darkness. It's 5 a.m., and we unload vegetables for awhile until reinforcements arrive in the form of Eric Barth, a young man who helps work the market for Tree and Leaf. They are soon carrying, sliding, and stacking crates of eggplant, radishes, kale, and more, and Zach is already making note of the need to talk to one of the interns back at the farm. "She didn't wash these radishes enough," he says. "The white part should be white-white." And he misses Katherine, yet again: "Every crate would have been labeled. Signage is my least favorite part."

For the next two hours, he and Eric pull the structure of the stand together, mostly working in tandem without even the need to talk. They set up tables, raise the tent—at 18 by 20 the stand is almost half the size of my nearby apartment—and start setting up boxes for the produce to spill out of, cornucopia-style. By 7 a.m., two more helpers have arrived and start arranging and stacking, as the market is coming to life around us.

How does he decide what to put where? Zach pauses. "There's so much to it," he says. "Mostly I want to show people things I'd like to move."

Meaning things he thinks they'll be into? He gives me a wry smile, and his eyes twinkle. I get it: Thinks he wants them to be into, right? He nods.

Generally, he wants the stand to look "incredibly abundant," and the piles should showcase the produce's "face," not stems. But that doesn't mean that once things are set up, he and his helpers just stand back and wait for customers. Zach stays in constant motion throughout the morning, arranging and rearranging, bunching and rebunching, stocking and restocking. This is not a touch of OCD at work; it's part of his philosophy that the atmosphere should seem lively. As a musician—he plays a melodic Irish drum called the bodhran—and a former actor, he doesn't mind the performance aspects of the market scene, but he prefers a subtler kind of showmanship. "Sometimes the display can be intimidating," he says. "You can see a customer maybe standing back, coming at it from the side, and you can make it less intimidating by just sorting through it in front of them. Or you can push out some smaller bunches. I try to read people."

He espouses an Irish style of customer service: friendly but not invasive. Moving around lets him easily chat with customers, answering questions and suggesting recipes. It can be a slow process, he says, educating urbanites who may not know their Tuscano from their Lacinato kale. And it falls to everyone, including his cashiers, such as Ariel Trahan, who says the queries do sometimes border on the silly. "My favorite questions are about size, like when people say, 'Last week your kale leaves were small and this week they're a little bigger. Is that a different variety?' I want to say, 'Think about it for a second.'"

But it's a two-way street. Soon after the market opens, and after Zach and I make a coffee run, a woman is asking him how much longer he'll have the Japanese Kamo eggplants. About two weeks, he says, and then she starts praising the variety's rich flavor and her favorite way to cook it: slowly roasted in a Dutch oven until it's "like custard." Another

customer says his favorite way to use the radishes—so often eaten raw—is to saute them in butter, to take the edge off the spicy bite, and to finish them with lemon juice and parsley.

Given all these radishes, which are so big some customers don't recognize them as radishes, Zach decides to go buy some salt nearby and set up helper Erin Vendahan with a knife and some paper plates for sampling. And it works. As soon as she starts slicing the watermelon radishes onto the plate, she pretty much stops traffic.

"Is that a turnip?" one woman asks.

"It's watermelon radish," Erin says. "Spicy and crunchy."

"I gotta taste that," the woman says, then pauses. "Is that supposed to taste like watermelon?"

Erin laughs: "It's supposed to taste like a radish."

When one customer comes in to inquire about Romano beans, those flat Italian green beans that are one of my favorites, too, Zach breaks the news: The germination rate was awful, probably because of the early summer heat. "I went with pole beans instead," he tells the man. "They're great, but they're not Romanos."

Such honesty has helped Zach earn regulars, and most seem to understand when the varieties or amounts he's growing change because of the vicissitudes of farming. That's why, even though sales have dipped since before the recession, he can still come away from a peak-summer weekend having sold $6,000 in produce at the Dupont market, and a little less at Falls Church. On this day, it's more like $4,000. Most years, the farm takes in about $225,000 in annual retail sales and another $40,000 wholesale. Zach wasn't comfortable going into any more detail, but suffice it to say that there are a lot of bills to pay, including that mortgage, and the margins are tight. That puts him in good company: According to the US Census Bureau, in 2009 more than 90 percent of American farms had sales of less than $249,000. Their average net earnings? Just $2,615.

Ann Yonkers, cofounder of FreshFarm Markets, which runs the Dupont venture and several others in and around the city, is proud of the role markets play in promoting small-scale agriculture. "There is simply no other way that small farms could sell what they grow and earn a premium for it," she told me. "The markets incubate farm businesses and enable them to grow as they figure out how to respond to demand."

Soon enough, the market is wrapping up, but Zach's day is far from over. Besides packing up, he has a two-hour drive back home, not including a stop at Potomac Vegetable Farms, where Hanna Newcomb operates one of the area's largest, and best, CSAs. For her 550 members, Newcomb's team grows vegetables on two farms and buys from three others, including Tree and Leaf. In addition to the vegetables Zach commits to selling her in advance, they also have an agreement that he can drop off what he doesn't sell at market and she'll buy it at an even lower price.

It's all part of the model that keeps Zach living up to the goal articulated in his farm's slogan, displayed on the big banner that's one of the last things to come down when he and his helpers dismantle the market stand when the last customer trickles out every Saturday and Sunday: "Cultivating sustainability from our farm to your table." Now that he's working his own soil rather than someone else's, the idea is full of new possibilities. "A few weeks ago a young guy read that sign and asked me: 'Sustainable practices, what does that really mean to you?' I said sustainable really means you can continue to do the same thing over and over again, and it might have a different form, but you're paying attention in a way that lets you continue. It means rebuilding the soil. It means realizing the astronomical implications of what you're doing."

He paused, and said emphatically, "It means realizing you have a lot of work to do."

# Chapter 4

# ON THE STOVETOP

Frankly, this is where I spend most of my time in the kitchen, and I bet you do, too: standing at the stove sautéing onions, stir-frying peppers and mushrooms, pan-frying cauliflower slices, or boiling pasta to finish in a quick pan sauce. And why not? Stovetop cooking is by far the most versatile, and it's this kind of cooking that leaves you feeling most in control because you can gauge just what's happening—dipping in for a taste, checking to see if something is tender or browned or both, stirring, lifting up and peeking, poking, bending your head close to the pot and inhaling the fragrant steam.

In fact, if I had to choose just two styles of dinner to make for myself from here to eternity, I would probably pick pasta and stir-fries. I do one or the other at least twice a week, if not more. My favorite pasta dishes are pure comfort food, and they come together in no longer than it takes to boil the dried pasta; I make the sauce simultaneously, and finish cooking the former in the latter. Stir-fries are even quicker, especially if I've already got the rice done, and there's no better way to make vegetables crisp-tender.

The best thing about making dinner on the stovetop is this: there's a good chance you can do the whole thing in one pan, building flavors and adding ingredients as you go. For us single cooks, who don't have the benefit of you-cook-and-I'll-clean partnerships, that means fewer dishes: a beautiful thing.

*When the corn is in peak season, I want to cook something that showcases that beautiful sweet flavor. This pasta recipe was inspired by the Southern tradition of creamed corn, which is made by getting that gorgeous milky pulp out of the corn (rather than adding cream to it), so that's what I do here. Combined with whole wheat pasta, fresh basil, and Pecorino cheese, the barely cooked corn sings a song of summer. If you feel like making this in the winter, I have one word for you: don't.*

# FUSILLI with CORN SAUCE

Bring a large pot of salted water to a boil and cook the pasta until it is al dente.

While the pasta is cooking, shuck the corn and rinse it under running water, removing as many of the silks as you can with your hands. Rub one of the ears over a coarse grater set over a bowl to catch the milk and pulp. Cut the kernels off the other cob with a knife (see page 180); keep the whole kernels separate from the milk and pulp.

Pour the oil into a large skillet set over medium heat. When the oil starts to shimmer, add the onion and garlic and sauté until tender. Add the corn kernels and sauté for just a few minutes, until the corn softens slightly and brightens in color. Stir in the corn milk and pulp and turn off the heat. Cover to keep warm.

When the pasta is al dente, drain it (reserving 1/2 cup of the pasta water) and add it to the skillet with the corn sauce. Toss to combine, adding a little pasta water if the sauce needs loosening. Stir in the cheese, then taste and add salt as needed and grind in plenty of fresh black pepper. Stir in the basil, scoop everything into a bowl, and eat.

3 ounces whole wheat fusilli, farfalle, or other curly pasta

2 ears fresh corn

1 tablespoon extra-virgin olive oil

1/2 large onion, chopped (about 3/4 cup)

1 clove garlic, thinly sliced

2 tablespoons freshly grated Pecorino Romano cheese

Sea salt

Freshly ground black pepper

4 fresh basil leaves, stacked, rolled, and thinly sliced

*Miso adds depth to roasted squash; here they make a quick pasta sauce (even quicker if you give the squash a head start in the microwave). Because you can't find squash much smaller than this, you'll end up with more squash flesh than you need for this recipe, but that's a bonus: refrigerate or freeze it and use it another time as the basis for a soup or side dish.*

# PASTA with SQUASH and MISO

Sprinkle the pumpkin seeds into a small skillet over medium-high heat. Cook, shaking the pan frequently, until the pumpkin seeds get golden brown in spots, turn fragrant, and start to pop (really!), a few minutes. Immediately transfer them to a plate to cool; if you leave them to cool in the pan, they can burn.

Preheat the oven to 400°F. Line a baking dish with aluminum foil, set the squash on it, and use a knife to poke several holes on every side of the squash. Roast it until a fork inserted into the flesh encounters no resistance, 45 minutes to an hour. Let cool. (Or first microwave the squash, after piercing it several times, on high for 3 minutes, then transfer it to the baking dish and roast for 25 to 35 minutes, until tender.) When the squash is cool enough to handle, cut it in half lengthwise and scoop out and discard the seeds and stringy matter. Use a spoon to remove the flesh from the skin; discard the skin. Reserve 1/2 cup of the flesh for this dish and refrigerate the remainder in an airtight container for up to 5 days, or freeze for up to 6 months.

Meanwhile, bring a large saucepan of salted water to a boil over medium-high heat. Add the pasta and cook according to the package directions, then drain (reserving 1/2 cup of the pasta water) and transfer it to a serving bowl.

In a small skillet over medium heat, heat the oil until it shimmers. Add the onion or shallot and sauté until it is soft and translucent. Add the miso, the 1/2 cup of squash flesh, and 1/2 cup of the reserved pasta cooking water, stirring to combine. Cook briefly just to let the flavors meld. Season with salt to taste; thin if needed with more pasta water.

Spoon the sauce over the pasta, tossing gently to work some of the sauce inside the pasta. Sprinkle with the pumpkin seeds and the Parmigiano-Reggiano, and eat.

1 **tablespoon unsalted shelled pumpkin seeds**

1 **small (12- to 16-ounce) butternut squash**

**Sea salt**

2 **ounces rigatoni, paccheri, or other large, tubular dried pasta**

1 **teaspoon extra-virgin olive oil**

1 **very small onion or large shallot lobe, chopped**

2 **teaspoons red miso**

2 **tablespoons freshly grated Parmigiano-Reggiano**

*You don't have to grow radishes to wonder why you so often see the bulbs sold in supermarkets alone, separated from their green tops, when both parts of the vegetable are so delicious. Thankfully, farmers' markets are a different story. Consider this treatment, in which the two parts of the plant come together. As much as I like raw radishes, they become sweeter and mellower if you cook them—like miniature versions of their relatives, the turnip.*

# SPAGHETTI with ROOT-TO-LEAF RADISH

Put a small, dry skillet over medium-low heat. Add the pine nuts and cook, shaking the pan and tossing the nuts frequently, until they are lightly browned and fragrant. Watch them carefully, and keep them moving, so they don't burn. Immediately transfer them to a plate to cool; if you leave them in the pan, even off the heat, they could burn.

Trim and scrub the radishes, and cut them from the greens. Discard any browned, wilted greens, keeping the freshest ones. Thoroughly wash them, but do not spin them dry. Cut the radishes in half, then into 1/4-inch-thick half-moons. Trim the long stems from the greens and thinly slice the stems. Stack the greens, roll them tightly, and slice them.

Bring a medium saucepan of salted water to a boil. Cook the spaghetti until it is slightly underdone, just shy of al dente, since it will cook further in the sauce.

Meanwhile, pour the olive oil into a medium skillet set over medium heat, and when the oil starts to shimmer add the anchovy and sauté briefly to let it flavor the oil, then add the garlic and onions and sauté until tender.

Stir in the sliced radishes, lower the heat to medium-low, cover, and cook until they have just started to become tender. Add the radish greens and cook just until they wilt.

When the pasta is ready, drain it (reserving 1/2 cup of the pasta water). Put the radish mixture over medium heat, add the spaghetti and lemon juice and zest, and toss and stir vigorously to combine, adding some of the pasta water if needed to create a creamy sauce. Taste, add salt, and grind a generous amount of black pepper on top. Transfer to a plate, sprinkle on the pine nuts and cheese, and eat.

- **2 tablespoons pine nuts**
- **4 red radishes with their greens (about 6 ounces)**
- **3 ounces farro spaghetti or whole wheat spaghetti**
- **2 teaspoons olive oil**
- **1 anchovy fillet, chopped (optional)**
- **1 clove garlic, chopped**
- **1 very small onion or large shallot lobe, thinly sliced**
- **2 tablespoons freshly squeezed lemon juice**
- **Grated zest of 1 lemon**
- **Sea salt**
- **Lots of freshly ground black pepper**
- **2 tablespoons grated Parmigiano-Reggiano**

*Risotto really isn't that hard to make; it comes together relatively quickly, and you don't actually have to stir constantly like you've always been told. Occasionally does the trick, as long as you add the hot liquid gradually so the grains swell and get creamy. If you don't have greens already made for this purpose, you can substitute 2 cups of fresh kale, collard greens, Swiss chard, beet greens, or a combination; strip the leaves from the stems, thoroughly wash and dry them, cut them into thin ribbons, and cook them with the zucchini. I like the addition of bitter radicchio to the mix, but you can leave it out if your tastes don't run that way.*

# RISOTTO with GREENS and ZUCCHINI

Pour 1 tablespoon of the olive oil into a small, heavy saucepan over medium heat. When it shimmers, add the zucchini or yellow squash and sauté until it barely starts to soften. Transfer the squash into a bowl.

Pour the vegetable stock into another small saucepan over medium-high heat. Bring to a boil, then reduce the heat to low, cover, and keep hot.

Return the saucepan to the heat and add the remaining 1 tablespoon of olive oil. When it shimmers, add the shallot and garlic and sauté until the vegetables are slightly soft. Stir in the rice and cook, stirring quickly, until the rice kernels are well coated. Pour in the wine and cook, stirring frequently, until the liquid is almost gone. Stir in the radicchio and 1/4 cup of the hot vegetable stock and cook, stirring occasionally, until the liquid is almost gone. Repeat with another 1/4 cup of the stock and continue cooking and stirring occasionally, being sure to scrape the bottom of the pan when you stir so the rice doesn't stick. Repeat until the rice has been cooking for about 20 minutes total. Taste to see if it is tender but still slightly firm to the bite.

Stir in the zucchini and the cooked greens and cook for another few minutes until the rice is tender but not mushy, adding a little more liquid to keep it very moist but not runny. When the rice is done to your liking, add the butter and cheese. Stir to combine, taste, and add more salt if necessary. Transfer to a shallow bowl, and eat.

2 tablespoons extra-virgin olive oil

1 small or 1/2 medium zucchini or yellow summer squash, cut into 1/2-inch cubes (about 1/2 cup)

1 to 1 1/2 cups vegetable stock (page 59) or water

1 shallot lobe, chopped

1 clove garlic, chopped

1/3 cup Arborio or other risotto rice

1/4 cup dry white wine

1/4 cup shredded radicchio (optional)

1/2 cup cooked greens (page 173), drained and chopped

2 teaspoons unsalted butter

2 tablespoons freshly grated Parmigiano-Reggiano

*One of my go-to takeout orders back in my meat-heavy days was fried rice with chopped shrimp. But when I shrunk it at home to single-serving size and also tried to accommodate my meatless eating using 1-inch pieces of baked tofu, something wasn't right—and it wasn't the lack of shrimp, I swear. I quickly realized that one of my favorite things about the dish (besides the hot-sour-spicy-sweet flavor, of course) was the fact that the shrimp pieces were really small, meaning every bite had a little blast of every flavor and texture in the dish. Once I chopped the baked tofu (which is less likely to fall apart than fresh, by the way), all was right with the world. By the way, in case you didn't know: don't use freshly made rice for fried rice, because it will get too mushy; day-old or frozen and thawed rice, however, is perfect.*

# SPICY BASIL TOFU FRIED RICE

Combine the soy sauce, water, and brown sugar in a small bowl, stirring to dissolve the sugar. Stem and seed the chile, discarding the stem but reserving the seeds. Chop the chile.

Heat the oil in a large skillet or wok over high heat, swirling to coat the sides. Add the chile and garlic and stir-fry until fragrant, about 20 seconds. Add the tofu and stir-fry until heated through and lightly colored, about 2 minutes.

Add the bell pepper, cooked rice, and soy sauce mixture; stir-fry until the bell pepper has started to soften and the liquid has evaporated, about 1 or 2 minutes. Quickly taste, and if you want the dish to be spicier, sprinkle in some of the reserved chile seeds. Add the basil and stir-fry just until it wilts, about 20 seconds. Garnish with basil and eat immediately.

1 teaspoon soy sauce

1 tablespoon water

1 teaspoon light brown sugar

1 small fresh Thai chile

2 teaspoons peanut oil

2 cloves garlic, chopped

3/4 cup Marinated and Baked Tofu (page 170) or store-bought baked tofu or pressed extra-firm tofu cubes, chopped small

1/2 small red bell pepper, stemmed, seeded and cut into 1/2-inch dice

3/4 cup brown (page 177) or white rice, preferably day-old or frozen and thawed

4 large basil leaves, rolled and thinly sliced, plus more for garnish

*When I tried Yotam Ottolenghi's pungently addictive black pepper tofu from his instant classic* Plenty, *I knew I'd recreate it downsized for one. What I ended up with is very different, since I treat the tofu like cutlets, and I added broccoli to bulk up the stir-fry base. Now, I have to admit, I'm addicted to my own version instead.*

# PEPPER-CRUSTED TOFU with BROCCOLI STIR-FRY

Wrap the drained tofu in paper towels, place on a plate, place a second plate on top and put a large unopened can of tomatoes or beans on top; let the tofu press for about 30 minutes. Unwrap, pat the tofu dry, and cut it into 2 or 3 half-inch-thick slices.

Working in a bowl, season the tofu on both sides with a light sprinkling of salt and a generous helping of black pepper, pressing the pepper in if needed so that it sticks. Use a small fine-mesh strainer to sift the cornstarch over the tofu a tablespoon or so at a time, turning the tofu and sifting again so the cornstarch coats it on both sides. Use your fingers if necessary to help thoroughly coat the tofu.

Into a large skillet, pour oil to a depth of 1/2 inch and set over medium heat. When the oil starts to shimmer, carefully add the tofu pieces and pan-fry them on both sides until golden brown and crisp. Transfer them to a cooling rack set over a plate or baking sheet to catch the oil.

While they are cooling, pour off all but a teaspoon or two of the vegetable oil and set the skillet over medium-high heat. Add the garlic, shallot, ginger, crushed red pepper, bell pepper, and broccoli and stir-fry until the broccoli and bell pepper are just barely tender. Stir in the green onion, soy sauce, 1/2 teaspoon of the sugar, and the water, then taste and add more sugar if needed. Transfer to a plate, top with the tofu, and eat.

6 ounces firm tofu, drained

Sea salt

Very coarsely ground black pepper

1/4 cup cornstarch

Vegetable oil

2 cloves garlic, thinly sliced

2 large shallot lobes, thinly sliced

1 tablespoon finely grated fresh ginger (from a peeled 2-inch piece)

1/4 teaspoon crushed red pepper flakes, or more if you want the dish particularly spicy

1/2 small red bell pepper, stemmed, cored, and thinly sliced

1 small broccoli crown, cut into small pieces

1 green onion, trimmed and thinly sliced

1 tablespoon light soy sauce

1/2 teaspoon sugar, plus more as needed

2 tablespoons water

*My sweet potato love—I call it my orange crush—is well documented. My last cookbook featured them in at least half a dozen ways. I often use them like this, along with leftover ingredients, to make a hash—in this case spiked with the funky spice of kimchi. No hash is complete without a poached egg, in my opinion, but obviously if you're vegan you can skip the egg.*

# SWEET POTATO, KIMCHI, and GREENS HASH

Bring a medium saucepan of water to a boil. Add the sweet potato cubes and boil until fork-tender. Drain and transfer them to a bowl to cool.

Pour 2 teaspoons of the oil into a small skillet over medium heat. When it shimmers, add the garlic, shallot, and crushed red pepper and sauté until the vegetables are tender. Scrape the mixture into the bowl with the sweet potato. Add the greens and kimchi and toss to combine. Taste and season with salt as needed.

Return the skillet to medium-high heat and pour in the remaining 1 teaspoon of oil. Add the hash, using a spatula to spread it evenly in the skillet and lightly pack it down. Cook it undisturbed for a few minutes, then peek underneath to see if it has browned. When it has, scrape it up with the spatula, stir it, and repack it. Repeat the scraping, stirring, and repacking a few times until the hash is nicely browned. Scoop it onto a plate, top with the poached egg, drizzle with a little Sriracha, and eat.

1 **very small sweet potato, peeled and cut into 1/2-inch cubes (about 3/4 cup)**

1 **tablespoon extra-virgin olive oil**

1 **clove garlic, thinly sliced**

1 **large shallot lobe, thinly sliced**

1/4 **teaspoon crushed red pepper flakes**

1/2 **cup cooked greens (page 173), squeezed of extra liquid and chopped**

1/4 **cup Cabbage Kimchi (page 163) or store-bought spicy kimchi, squeezed of extra liquid and chopped**

1 **Perfect Poached Egg (page 17)**

**Sriracha (optional)**

*I was at the delightful Dirt Candy restaurant in New York, marveling at a dish of fried, smoked cauliflower, when I realized I should make a chicken-fried version of the same. I'm a chicken-fried steak fan from way back; it was the first thing I learned to make as a kid in West Texas. But now that I am moving past my steak-eating days, I knew I could get my fix from a sturdy vegetable like cauliflower, cut into a single thick slice like a chop. Serve this with grits, polenta, or mashed potatoes and braised greens. And don't worry about the fact that you'll have left-over cauliflower when you make a big cut out of the center like I call for here. Just break up the remaining vegetable into florets, roast at 500 degrees with a generous amount of olive oil and coarse sea salt, and toss it into salads and pasta dishes for days to come.*

# CHICKEN-FRIED CAULIFLOWER with MISO-ONION GRAVY

Set the cauliflower slice in a medium skillet (preferably just big enough to hold it) over medium heat and pour in ¼ inch of water. When the water starts to bubble, reduce the heat to medium-low, cover, and gently steam the cauliflower until it just starts to feel tender when you pierce it with a fork, about 10 minutes. Carefully transfer the cauliflower to a plate to cool, then sprinkle it with salt on both sides.

Put the egg and flour in separate wide, shallow bowls or plates. Stir the paprika, ground chile, and a little more salt into the flour. Dip the cauliflower in egg on both sides, then dredge it in the flour mixture, using a spoon or your fingers as needed to coat it as thoroughly as possible in the flour. (If the cauliflower breaks up, just dredge and fry the pieces.)

Pour the water out of the skillet, return it to medium heat, and pour in ¼ inch of canola oil. When the oil starts to shimmer, gently lay the cauliflower in and fry it until it is golden brown and crisp, then turn it over and repeat on the other side. Transfer the cauliflower to a plate lined with a paper towel.

Pour off all but a scant teaspoon of the oil, return the skillet to medium-low heat, and add the onions, miso, and ¼ cup of water. Cook, stirring to thoroughly combine, until the mixture forms a sauce, adding more water if needed.

Transfer the cauliflower to a plate, spoon the gravy on top, and eat.

1 thick (1-inch) slice cauliflower, from the center of a large, trimmed head

Sea salt

1 egg, lightly whisked

¼ cup flour

¼ teaspoon Spanish smoked paprika (pimentón)

¼ teaspoon ground ancho or other chile

Canola oil, for frying

2 tablespoons Caramelized Onions (page 166)

2 teaspoons white miso

You may not have known this, but the word *enchiladas* comes from the Spanish verb for covering in chiles, which is what happens with the corn tortillas in that classic Mexican dish. You Spanish speakers get where I'm going with this: *enfrijoladas*, then, means tortillas enrobed in . . . beans! These are traditionally topped rather than filled, and they're not baked. All of which makes them so easy—particularly when you've got some home-cooked beans just waiting for their next use—that, well, you may not go back to enchiladas again. Not that you have to choose, of course. By the way, even though I call for pinto or black beans to keep things in the Mexican spirit, you could make these with any of your favorites: cannellini, an heirloom variety such as Jacob's Cattle, even black-eyed peas or chickpeas. You can experiment with other toppings: pickled onions, chopped tomatoes, salsa, and/or thinly sliced cabbage.

# ENFRIJOLADAS with EGG, AVOCADO, and ONION

Warm the tortillas by heating them in a dry skillet over medium-low heat until they are pliable. Wrap them in a packet of aluminum foil to keep them warm while you make the sauce.

Pour the oil into a large skillet over medium heat. Reserve 1 teaspoon of onion for the garnish, and when the oil shimmers, add the remaining onion and the garlic to the skillet and sauté until tender. Sprinkle in the ancho chile, cumin, and cayenne, stir to combine, and let the spices sizzle and bloom for a few seconds. Stir in the beans and the bean liquid.

Bring the beans to a simmer, then mash them in the skillet with a fork or potato masher. Taste and add salt and more cayenne as needed. Cook until the beans are slightly thickened but still fairly loose, the texture of very thick soup.

Using tongs, immerse the warm tortillas in the sauce to coat, then take them out and fold or roll them; transfer them to a plate and spoon the rest of the sauce on top. Sprinkle with the reserved onion, chopped egg, feta, and avocado, and eat.

2 (6-inch) or 3 smaller corn tortillas

1 tablespoon extra-virgin olive oil

1 very small onion or large shallot lobe, finely chopped

2 cloves garlic, finely chopped

1/2 teaspoon ground ancho chile (page 112)

1/2 teaspoon ground cumin

Pinch of cayenne (optional), plus more as needed

3/4 cup cooked cooked black or pinto beans (page 175) or rinsed canned beans, drained

3/4 cup bean cooking liquid or water

Sea salt

1 Perfectly Creamy Hard-Cooked Egg (page 167), chopped

2 tablespoons feta or queso fresco, crumbled

1/2 avocado, cubed

## Grind Your Own

"Chili powder" is one of the biggest misnomers in the supermarket spice aisle. You'd think that it's synonymous with ground chile peppers of some kind, wouldn't you? And you'd be wrong. It usually includes cumin and garlic and salt and, in some cases, silicon dioxide (noted on the ingredient list for its ability to keep the mixture "free flowing"). But when I want a hit of chile pepper flavor, that's all I want, and I prefer to add the other spices and seasonings separately, depending on the dish. So I prefer ground ancho chile, which you can find in Latin markets and at good spice stores such as Penzeys.

But since chile peppers, like other spices, start to lose their potency as soon as they are ground, you can also easily make your own. Toast 2 or 3 dried ancho chile peppers in a dry skillet over medium heat, turning periodically, until they are brown all over. Let cool, remove the stems, and use a dedicated electric spice grinder (such as an old coffee grinder) to pulverize them to a powder. (If you want the powder to be less spicy, discard the seeds from the pepper before grinding.) Transfer to a small airtight container and store as you would any spice: in a cool, dry place.

*I've loved tostadas since my West Texas youth, when I would get them at Tex-Mex restaurants anytime I wasn't ordering enchiladas. At home, they may seem a little fussy to make for a single serving, but you can speed things up by using ingredients that you've already cooked: the beans, of course, but even potatoes you've preboiled (or roasted) in bigger batches. You can also buy tostadas or fry up a dozen tortillas at a time, keeping them in an airtight container for a few days and breaking up some into soups or onto salads if, unlike me, you don't want tostadas multiple days in a row. If you'd like, you can use Smoky Bean and Roasted Garlic Dip (page 152) instead of the whole beans.*

# POTATO and BEAN TOSTADAS with AVOCADO–GREEN ONION SALSA

Bring a medium saucepan of salted water to a simmer and add the potato. Cook until barely tender, 6 to 8 minutes, then drain.

While the potato is boiling, combine the avocado in a small bowl with the green onion, lime juice, honey, jalapeño, and cilantro. Taste and add salt as needed.

Sprinkle the pumpkin seeds into a small skillet over medium-high heat. Cook, shaking the pan frequently, until the pumpkin seeds get golden brown in spots, turn fragrant, and start to pop, a few minutes. Immediately transfer them to a plate to cool; if you leave them to cool in the pan, they can burn.

Into a large skillet, pour oil to a depth of 1/4 inch and set over medium heat. When the oil starts to shimmer, add the tortillas in a single layer, being careful not to crowd them and working in batches if needed, and pan-fry them on both sides until golden brown and crisp. Use tongs or a slotted spatula to transfer them to a paper towel–lined plate to drain.

Increase the heat to medium-high and add the boiled potato cubes. Fry them until golden brown and crisp on two sides, then use a slotted spoon to transfer them to another paper towel–lined plate to drain. While the potatoes are still hot, sprinkle them with a little salt and with the smoked paprika and cayenne.

Lay the tostadas out onto a plate. Divide the beans and potatoes among the tostadas. Top with the avocado salsa, sprinkle with the pumpkin seeds, and eat with your hands.

1 small (5-ounce) potato, scrubbed but not peeled, cut into 1-inch cubes

1/2 avocado, cut into 1/2-inch cubes

2 green onions, trimmed and thinly sliced

1 tablespoon freshly squeezed lime juice

1/2 teaspoon honey

1/2 jalapeño, stemmed, seeded, and chopped

2 tablespoons chopped cilantro leaves

Sea salt

2 tablespoons unsalted shelled pumpkin seeds

Vegetable oil

2 or 3 (6-inch) corn tortillas

1/2 teaspoon smoked paprika

Pinch of ground cayenne pepper (optional)

1/2 cup room temperature pinto or black beans, homemade (page 175) or canned, drained and rinsed

*When I want to dig into thicker, meatier pieces of eggplant, I like to steam it, which helps break down the spongy flesh into a beautifully soft texture without making it totally collapse. Tomato sauce might seem out of place in a recipe with the flavors of miso, ginger, and sesame, but it works. With udon standing in for linguini, this dish gets a treatment that walks the line between Asian and Italian, just like eggplant itself.*

# STEAMED EGGPLANT with MISO-TOMATO SAUCE

Sprinkle the peanuts into a small skillet over medium-high heat. Cook, shaking the pan frequently, until the peanuts darken and become fragrant. Immediately transfer them to a plate to cool; if you leave them to cool in the pan, they can burn. Once they are cool, chop them.

Lightly salt the eggplant rounds and put them into a steamer basket set into a pot with an inch or so of water in it. Place the pot over medium heat, cover, and steam until the eggplant is very soft but still holds its shape, 20 to 30 minutes.

Pour the sesame oil into a small skillet over medium heat. When it starts to shimmer, add the ginger and sauté until tender. Whisk the miso and vinegar together until smooth, then add to the skillet. Stir in the tomato sauce. Cook for just a few minutes to allow the flavors to meld.

Meanwhile, cook the udon noodles in a saucepan of boiling water according to the package directions, usually about 8 minutes, until they are silky but retain a little bit of chewiness, and drain.

When the eggplant is tender, pile the noodles into a shallow serving bowl, top with the eggplant slices, and spoon on the sauce. Sprinkle with the green onion and peanuts, and eat.

2 tablespoons raw unsalted peanuts

1 small (6- to 8-ounce) Asian or Italian eggplant, unpeeled and cut into 1-inch rounds

Sea salt

2 teaspoons toasted sesame oil

1 (1-inch) piece fresh ginger, peeled and finely chopped

2 tablespoons white miso

2 teaspoons rice vinegar, preferably unseasoned

3/4 cup Tomato Sauce with a Kick (page 176) or store-bought tomato sauce

3 ounces dried udon noodles

1 green onion, trimmed and thinly sliced

One of the first tofu concoctions I fell for is the traditional version of this mapo-style dish, which I had at Great Wall Szechuan House in Washington's Logan Circle. With its numbing Szechuan peppercorns and fatty ground pork (or beef), it's the first love of other, much more tofu-versed cooks than I, too. Andrea Nguyen, for one, waxes poetic about it in her book Asian Tofu, and offers a dynamite recipe. But it wasn't until after I visited her and she gave me a little plastic baggie full of chile bean sauce from the Pixian region of China, scooping it from a beautiful, multicolored, paper-lined package, that I tried to make the dish myself. Or, I should say, a vegetarian, shrunk-to-single-serving interpretation of the dish. If you have access to a great Asian market, look for Pixian chile bean sauce (let Andrea's fabulous Asian Market Shopper smartphone app guide you). If you don't, a chile garlic paste will suffice. The all-important Szechuan peppercorns are available at such markets and also at online spice purveyors such as Penzeys.

# SZECHUAN-STYLE TOFU and SHIITAKE STIR-FRY

Sprinkle the peppercorns into a small skillet set over medium heat and toast them until they are very fragrant and slightly darkened. Let them cool slightly, then smash them in a mortar and pestle or under a cast-iron skillet on the countertop.

Have all your ingredients ready near the stove, as the stir-fry goes quickly.

Pour the oil into a wok or large skillet over high heat. Add the mushrooms and stir-fry until they collapse, about 2 minutes. Add the ginger and chile bean sauce and stir-fry until the mushrooms and oil have turned red from the sauce. Stir in the sugar and soy sauce, and then the tofu. Pour in 1/2 cup of water, bring to a vigorous simmer, and cook for a few minutes to heat the tofu through and allow it to absorb the flavors.

Taste, add more soy sauce or sugar if needed, and stir in the green onion and the dissolved cornstarch to slightly thicken the sauce. Eat hot over rice.

1/2 teaspoon Szechuan peppercorns

1 tablespoon canola or peanut oil

1 cup shiitake mushrooms, stemmed and chopped

1 teaspoon finely chopped fresh ginger

1 tablespoon chile bean sauce

1/2 teaspoon sugar

1/2 teaspoon soy sauce

1 cup Marinated and Baked Tofu (page 170) or store-bought baked or extra-firm tofu, cut into 1/2-inch cubes

1 green onion, trimmed and thinly sliced

1 teaspoon cornstarch dissolved in 1 tablespoon water

1/2 cup warm cooked brown rice (page 177) or other grain

*When I tried to recreate a beautiful winter squash curry dish I had at Thai Crossing in Washington's LeDroit Park neighborhood, I just couldn't get it quite right. It tasted too watery. And then I realized that I was using the wrong kind of squash. Once I switched to the drier kabocha, which absorbs the coconut curry rather than leaking out diluting juices, I knew I had a winner: a creamy, hearty, soul-satisfying dinner. If you can't find kabocha, buttercup and acorn are decent substitutes.*

# THAI-STYLE KABOCHA SQUASH and TOFU CURRY

Peel the squash, remove the stem, cut it in half, and scoop out the seeds. Cut one of the halves in half again, and use that for this dish, reserving the rest for another use.

Pour the oil into a medium saucepan over medium-high heat. When it shimmers, add the shallot, ginger, and curry paste and cook, stirring, for just a minute or so. Stir in the broth and coconut milk and bring to a boil, then lower the heat until the liquid is barely bubbling around the edges. Add the squash and tofu pieces, cover, and cook until the squash is tender, about 15 to 20 minutes. Taste and add salt as needed.

Stir in the basil leaves, spoon the mixture over rice, top with bean sprouts, and eat.

- 1 medium (2-pound) kabocha squash
- 1 tablespoon extra-virgin olive oil
- 2 large shallot lobes, cut into $1/2$-inch chunks
- 1 (1-inch) piece fresh ginger, peeled and grated
- $1/2$ to 1 tablespoon Thai red curry paste
- $1/2$ cup vegetable broth or water
- $2/3$ cup light coconut milk
- $1/2$ cup Marinated and Baked Tofu (page 170)

  Sea salt
- 4 large basil leaves, stacked, rolled, and thinly sliced
- $1/2$ cup warm cooked brown rice (page 177) or other grain
- 2 tablespoons bean sprouts (optional)

*Some cooks will find this practically blasphemous, but I think there's something overrated about green beans that have been barely cooked. You know, that crisp-tender treatment that has become the standard? I often find myself wishing they were a little less crisp and a little more tender, so those grassy flavors would turn deeper and rounder. I guess it's my Southern heritage, because we have long known that there is something special about the flavor of green beans that have been long cooked. This dish also happens to be perfect for the wintertime, because it works with frozen beans, too. If you'd like to add a little protein to this meal, a poached egg (page 17) or Marinated and Baked Tofu (page 170) would be a natural.*

# TOMATO-BRAISED GREEN BEANS and NEW POTATOES

Choose a small skillet for which you have a tight-fitting lid, and place it over medium-high heat. Add the green beans, tomato sauce, and enough water so the beans are barely covered. Top with the potatoes.

Let the mixture come to a boil, then reduce the heat until it is simmering. Cover and cook until the potatoes are tender and the green beans are very soft with no trace of crispness, about 30 minutes, stirring a few times and adding water if the pan seems too dry. Add the salt, pepper, honey, and vinegar, taste, and add more of any of them to achieve the sweet-and-sour balance you like. Sprinkle with parsley and eat.

8 ounces flat Romano or other green beans, trimmed (may substitute frozen)

1 cup Tomato Sauce with a Kick (page 176) or store-bought sauce plus a pinch of crushed red pepper flakes

4 or 5 very small new potatoes (about 4 ounces total), scrubbed well and halved

1/2 teaspoon sea salt, plus more to taste

1/2 teaspoon freshly ground black pepper, plus more to taste

1 teaspoon honey, plus more to taste

1 teaspoon red wine vinegar, plus more to taste

2 tablespoons chopped fresh parsley leaves

# WHEN PARADISE GETS PAVED

You could cover the whole earth with asphalt,
but sooner or later green grass would break through.

—**ILYA EHRENBURG,** *Boris Leonidovich Pasternak*, 1921

My sister Rebekah taught me something long ago: if you want the truth, listen to Joni Mitchell. Joni's heyday may have been a little before my time, but once I started listening I caught up quickly. And sure enough, among many other pieces of wisdom that feel truer and truer the older I get, there's this classic: "You don't know what you've got till it's gone."

Of course, merely hearing those words, or even singing along to them, wasn't enough for them to sink in. I still squandered the promise of too many romantic relationships, for instance, because I thought something better would come along—and for a long while, it did. Until it didn't. More recently, though, Joni's words have been ringing in my ears every time I look out the window. I'm not mourning a lost relationship this time. What I miss is soil. Last year, my view included my sister and brother-in-law's homestead garden in southern Maine, but this year in Washington all I can see from my dining-room window is an urban alleyway in the foreground and a classical Masonic temple in the background.

A half-dozen years ago, when I lived in Jamaica Plain, which has become the Brooklyn of Boston, I took my backyard for granted, crowding it with grills and smokers and patio furniture, letting my dog use it for his business, and always telling myself, and my downstairs neighbors, that I'd plant something there someday. I never managed more than a few pitiful hostas, but on my front balcony I did cultivate containers full of basil, mint, parsley, cilantro, thyme, oregano, and rosemary. As a single cook, I relished the ability, for a few short months a year, to avoid buying those clamshell packs of herbs in the supermarket.

Then I moved to DC in 2006, and my list of four must-haves in a condo—proximity to work, affordability, dog-friendliness, and outdoor space—had to shrink to three. I sold the grilling gear and took my pooch to a nearby dog park for romping. And soon enough, I couldn't stop thinking about the garden I'd never have. In my new apartment, there wasn't even a big enough windowsill for potted herbs, let alone anything more ambitious.

Just a week after moving in, though, I was walking down 15th Street less than two blocks from my new home, when behind that Masonic temple I saw it: a sign that said "Temple Garden" sticking up above a line of shrubs. Behind it was a half-block square of green, and from the sidewalk I could see sprawling tomato plants, tall bushes of rosemary, sunflowers towering above all. I opened the little iron gate (no locks here) and took a walk around. Nobody was tending a plot at the time, so I followed the neat mulch-covered paths, labeled with names like Raspberry Row and Lavender Lane, past eggplant, chard, kale, peppers, basil, and more, including so many plants I didn't even recognize. I knew it immediately: this community garden would be my savior.

A visit to the website and an email exchange first raised my hopes, then burst my bubble. Yes, there were seventy plots, but also an eighty-person waiting list, getting longer every year because of the growing number of people interested in growing food. And the turnover was only about fifteen to twenty plots a year, usually because people move out of the zip codes required for membership. You don't have to be good at math to see how long that could take, but no other community gardens were near me, and no others had openings, either. I put my name in.

That was 2006. In 2009, I got the nod. It was July, and someone had left their plot midseason; it was at the intersection of paths that were named, amusingly, Hollywood and Vine. I enlisted my coworker and friend Jane Black, another single cook with more interest than experience in gardening, to split the sweat equity and whatever meager bounty might result.

We fumbled around. I had gotten some good firsthand lessons in gardening over the previous several years from Rebekah and my brother-in-law, Peter, who are trying to grow, and put up, enough food to sustain themselves year-round with minimal other food purchases. But my attention was admittedly sporadic. I had certainly never put my sister's lessons into practice, and Jane and I both suffered from one of the most problematic conditions that can befall gardeners: impatience. It took me two days of solid work just to pull out all the wild fennel the previous gardener had left behind, but then we took some shortcuts, especially when it came to soil prep and weeding. We muddled through, planted a quirky mix, started much of it too late to get very far that summer, and then proceeded to forget that we should be thinking about the fall as well. And we disagreed on some things. Should we devote so much space to four mountain-strawberry plants just because

I became enamored of them at a farmers' market stand? We wouldn't get berries until the second year, and even then, not many. But think of it. Our own strawberries! Jane wanted more flowers, and I wanted more jalapeños.

Things went better the next summer, thanks in no small part to a spring visit from Rebekah, who put in a day of work herself. We were going to just do a little weeding, a little planting, but after I read the look on my sister's face as she sifted through the dusty dirt, still filled with too many rocks and roots, I said, "You think we should just start over, and prepare the soil some more, don't you?" And so we did, sifting and weeding and adding compost and mulch. Jane and I got plenty of other advice from her and fellow Temple Gardeners, all of them wiser than us by far, and learned to prune young tomato plants so they would set more fruit, to water them gently at the base to prevent mold, and to weed, weed, weed, and weed some more. Like fledgling gardeners everywhere, we found some things that grew well and we liked to eat (Sungold cherry tomatoes), some that grew well but we didn't like (gorgeous—and flavorless—pineapple sage),

and some that we liked but couldn't really get to take hold (squash).

We learned that a little theft problem could be thwarted by picking the tomatoes just before they ripen and by growing Green Zebras and those yellow cherries, varieties that hungry neighbors seemed to pass over. And I started sprinkling coffee grounds around the base of those tomatoes to thwart nonhuman invaders. Then Jane, having met the man who would become her husband, started to drift away and eventually moved. I struggled at times to juggle the demands of weeding and watering and planting with yet another commitment: a cookbook project. Still, we grew Thai chile peppers that I chopped into fish sauce for a condiment, sparse amounts of other peppers and carrots, herbs (of course), and, at one point at least, almost more Sungolds than we could handle.

By the third season, now without Jane, I had settled into something of a rhythm. I was reaching nothing close to the output of Peter and Rebekah, but I squeaked a few meals out of the plot here and there. I had devoted a third of the garden over the winter to garlic, pressing the little cloves into the soil the previous fall and covering it with straw, and it bounded up in the spring to greet me. I didn't grow corn or lima beans—my plot had far too little space for those—but as soon as both appeared at the farmers' market I would use my own basil, tomatoes, and squash to make succotash, a dish that, like gazpacho and Caprese salad, tells me it's summer.

More importantly, I would stop by the garden on my way to or from work, or both, punctuating my office-bound days with a dose of

weeding or watering or mulching or harvesting. Even if I only had twenty minutes, it was my time to clear my head, focus, and think about something other than the unanswered emails that awaited me at work.

Just as I had started to find a groove, though, we gardeners were dealt a blow worse than any stinkbug or sticky-fingered thief. The Masons own the land, and they announced that they would close the twenty-one-year-old garden in November so they could stage construction equipment for a rehab project on their century-old temple. You can't make this stuff up: paradise was about to be paved (or at least ripped up) so they could put up a parking lot (of sorts). The garden's officers tried to change the Masons' minds. We held an open house, organized a letter-writing campaign, started Facebook and Twitter outreach. One of my Tweets quoted the Ben Franklin version of the Joni Mitchell sentiment: "When the well's dry, we know the worth of water."

During the campaign, I couldn't stop thinking about a particular set of gardeners on the other side of the country who had used more aggressive tactics than we did when they were faced with closure. In South Central Los Angeles in the early-2000s, the largest of the country's 25,000 community gardens was threatened after the city decided to sell it back to the previous owner in a backroom deal. That drama, documented in the Oscar nominated film *The Garden*, involved lawsuits and broken promises and racial politics, and it climaxed in rage and despair and the revving of bulldozer engines. The differences between their situation and ours, of course, were stark: our little garden consisted of seventy-something tiny plots on a mere quarter-acre, in a gentrified neighborhood, while the South Central garden included hundreds of plots on a whopping fourteen acres amid gritty warehouses, and it served more than 300 mostly Latino families. While we grew everything from kale and tomatoes to squash and berries, in Southern California, avocado trees shared space with guavas and papayas and multicolored corn. Both gardens, of course, served urbanites who didn't have access to outdoor space but longed to dig and water and prune and harvest. But many of the South Central garden's *campesinos* depended on the garden for their very sustenance.

Politically speaking, the South Central gardeners had every right to protest. The land was given to them by the city after the Rodney King riots, and what the city giveth, the city taketh away. With no warning or public discussion, the city council sold the land back to owner Ralph Horowitz for the same exact price, $5 million, that he had been paid twenty years earlier when the city seized the property by eminent domain. Horowitz claimed he was entitled to repurchase the land because the city didn't follow through on its original plan (to build a trash incinerator); the community squashed those plans, and in the void the garden sprung up. The city council ended up agreeing with Horowitz. Anyone who has tended anything for very long could feel the gardeners' pain; and at one of their first organizing meetings to fight the decision, the sense of outrage was palpable: more than one wore a beret, and more than one cried "Viva Zapata!"

We Temple Gardeners were plenty angry, and sad, too, but for us there was a clear sense that, ultimately, the Masons had every right to use their land however they deemed fit, even if we thought they were terribly wrong to decide they had to uproot the garden and not the pristine lawn next to it. There were no claims of injustice as there had been in Los Angeles in 2006, or in East London in 2012, when the century-old Manor Garden allotments were demolished to make room for the Olympics. The Masons politely notified us in plenty of time for us to try our public awareness campaign and to start making other plans. They met with our officers, and they heard our counterproposals: put the equipment on the adjacent lawn instead (we would help resod it afterward); or if that wasn't possible, close just part of the garden (it would help provide a buffer between the construction and the street); or if that wasn't possible, at least make the closure temporary and let us come back postconstruction. The Masons responded to our strong-but-polite pleas with a firm-but-polite answer: no.

So 2011 was the last year I had those Sungolds to roast and stir into risotto. I was tempted to uproot my three-year-old oregano, which was flowering gloriously, and the strawberries, and the basil I like to make into a paste and freeze, and the fall spinach from my sister's saved-by-hand seeds, and the lemon balm and the shiso and the tarragon and the golden beets, and to find them all another home. But as the closing date approached, I couldn't bring myself to do it. I couldn't even bring myself to attend any of the farewell parties thrown by fellow gardeners. Aside from some cleanup duties we all agreed to help with, I stopped going to my plot. I just couldn't face it.

The garden had become more than just a place to grow food, as important as that was. Other gardeners at Temple, as in South Central Los Angeles and London and all over the world have long known that these urban oases are places where neighbors socialize, where they learn from one another, and where they go to escape the cars and the concrete among others as interested in the soil as they are. Sure, I missed the gardening, but I started to realize that perhaps I missed the community even more. And then, just as the garden fight was ending, my beloved Doberman died suddenly and shockingly. My other main connection to the community—the dog park where I took Red every day to run with the other pooches while I socialized—was severed, too.

Between those losses and a touch of work exhaustion, I needed a change of pace. Inspired by my time at Temple, I decided to spend a year living with my sister, learning firsthand how she and her husband manage to coax so much to eat out of their 8,000 square feet of growing space in Maine. The work was hard; I spent countless hours shoveling manure, gathering seaweed, spreading mulch, planting, transplanting, replanting, killing bugs by hand, and, finally, harvesting and cooking and preserving. Once the crops started coming in, I got plenty spoiled by this escape from the tyranny of the supermarket, this ability to go pick just as much as I wanted or needed—or, at some points, as much as the plant demanded. But as much as I enjoyed it, as much as I was learning, I felt anxious every time I thought about returning to Washington without my little plot and my fellow gardeners to help sustain me. Just as I was picking up so many ideas about how to garden effectively, I started realizing that my own personal drought was on the way.

Six months after we had to be out of the Temple Garden, I started getting reports from friends back in Washington that the land was just sitting there, untouched. Weeds had overtaken many of the plots, but kale and collards and broccoli, among other things, had overwintered. It was infuriating, of course. I immediately wondered if my strawberry plants had survived, or if someone had taken them to use elsewhere. It wasn't until June that a friend texted me a photo showing that what was supposed to have happened the previous fall was finally happening, without fanfare: a bulldozer was smoothing over the land. He wrote: "Garden is gone. :-(" I couldn't think of what else to say, so I just wrote "Saddest pic ever."

I thought of *The Garden*, and how in 2009, three years after the city sold back the land to the previous owner, three years after the protesters chanted and the bulldozers came, the land remained undeveloped. I remembered the conversation I had at the time with the film's director and one of the gardeners. The resignation was apparent in their voices. "The urgency of removing people was false," organizer Rufina Juarez, who has a starring role in the documentary, told me. "All this hurrying up was not true."

At the end of *The Garden*, the (literally) crushing disappointment that comes when the bulldozers knock down fences and plow through corn plants taller than the Caterpillars themselves lifts, at least a little. We learn that some of the *campesinos* have found other places to farm. Juarez is among those who started an eighty-acre farm near Bakersfield, and they truck their produce to the city to sell it at farmers' markets; they even have a CSA subscription program. Their current acreage is more than five times that of their land in South Central, so in our interview I had to ask her: didn't things maybe, actually, end up working out for the better?

"I don't think it's better," she said. "The piece that's missing, that's vital, is that urban gardens allow for communities to grow, so there's an exchange. That piece is difficult to get at the farmers' market. Providing access to an area that has a need is still an issue."

As soon as the Masons announced their intention to close the Temple Garden, our group started trying to find another piece of land, too. Several possibilities emerged, including a new community garden on the property of a nearby church. This garden's primary mission would be to provide produce for families in need, and connections were being made to the organizations that serve them, but the gardeners would be entitled to some produce for themselves, too. Suddenly, it seemed possible that two missions might converge into one, as they had in Los Angeles.

I emailed the organizers that as soon as I returned to DC, I wanted in. And I knew that this time, I wouldn't take a thing—not a stubborn weed, not a stolen tomato, and certainly not the community—for granted.

## Chapter 5

# SWEETS

Most of what passes for dessert in my kitchen, when I'm cooking for my three favorite people—me, myself, and I—can usually be held in my hands, because it's a piece of fruit. Or I get all adventurous and . . . stir jam into yogurt and top it with some nuts. But the thing is, I love to bake, which means that sometimes I just can't help myself, and have to make a batch of cookies, or at least layer some crumbled ones under some sweetened yogurt with that fruit and those nuts on top.

The surprise to those who haven't gone there yet is this: you don't have to bake for a crowd every time you bake. You don't have to supply your officemates with the rest of your batch of three dozen cookies when you had a hankering for just one. Don't get me wrong: sharing is a lovely thing to do, but it's not your only option. With a little planning (and the use of your freezer), you can make a large batch of dough but bake just what you want, no more.

Sure, it might seem indulgent to make dessert for yourself, but think about it: isn't indulgence the point of dessert, anyway?

*I was at Palena, my favorite restaurant in Washington, at the end of a sublime meal, when the dessert's taste and texture made me gasp. It was a shallow lemon custard, not just silky but crystal clear in its flavor: a blast of lemon, cream, and sugar in one bite. Pastry chef Aggie Chin explained that it's her take on posset, a traditional English dessert in which the cream softly sets with nothing but the help of the acid from the lemon juice. I knew I'd try this at home. It makes the perfect topping for the cookie-crumble crust I like to make (as in the "tart" on page 130 and the Faux Tart pictured opposite), and the perfect base for the fruit I like best with lemons: berries. This can be easily doubled when you'd like to make dessert for two nights in a row, or for you and a friend to share.*

# FAUX TART with INSTANT LEMON GINGER CUSTARD

Sprinkle the crumbled cookie into the bottom of a large ramekin, small glass jar, or small shallow bowl. Drizzle the crumbs with honey, then use a fork to combine the two and then to lightly pack down the mixture. Transfer to the freezer while you make the custard.

Grate the ginger, then press the grated ginger through a fine-mesh strainer into a small bowl. You should have about a teaspoon of ginger juice.

Pour the cream into a small saucepan set over medium heat, stir in the sugar, and bring the mixture to a boil. Let it boil for about 5 minutes, then remove from the heat and stir in the ginger juice and lemon juice. Let the mixture cool in the saucepan for about 20 minutes.

Pour the warm cream mixture into the ramekin over the crumbs, and refrigerate until the cream has set, at least 30 minutes but possibly longer, depending on the depth of the container and the fat content of the cream. (Or you can make it the day before; cover it with a piece of plastic wrap pressed tightly on the surface of the cream.) The custard will be softly set, like a pudding, not firm like a flan.

Top with the berries and eat.

1 or 2 gingersnap cookies, crumbled (about 1/3 cup of crumbs)

1 teaspoon honey

1 (2-inch) piece fresh ginger, peeled

1/2 cup heavy cream

2 tablespoons sugar

3 tablespoons freshly squeezed lemon juice

A handful of blackberries, blueberries, or raspberries

*Here's why I use those quotation marks: this can't really be a tart because there's no baking. Instead, when it's hot out and I can't be bothered to turn on the oven, I use a cookie (store bought or homemade), crumbled and bound with some honey, as the crust. Instead of cooked pastry cream, it's barely sweetened thick yogurt, topped with berries. And I build it in a small glass jar or ramekin for ease of preparation and consumption.*

# SUMMER BERRY "TART" IN A JAR

Sprinkle the almonds into a small skillet over medium-high heat. Cook, shaking the pan frequently, until the almonds have darkened and become fragrant, just a few minutes. Immediately transfer them to a plate to cool; if you leave them to cool in the pan, they can burn.

In a small bowl, mix the cookie crumbs with ½ teaspoon of the honey. Scrape the mixture into a ramekin or squat ½-pint glass jar, and pack it down evenly to form a crust. In the same bowl, whisk together the yogurt, almond extract, and the remaining ½ teaspoon honey. Spoon it into the ramekin or jar, top with the berries and almonds, and eat.

1 tablespoon sliced or slivered almonds

1 chocolate cookie, crumbled or smashed (about ¼ cup of crumbs)

1 teaspoon honey

½ cup plain fat-free Greek-style yogurt (may substitute low-fat or whole)

½ teaspoon almond or vanilla extract

¼ cup blackberries, raspberries, blueberries, or a mixture

# More Ideas for Tarts in Jars

Follow the procedure for Summer Berry "Tart" in a Jar (page 130), with these combinations.

**Nutty Chocolate Tart:**
*Base:* peanut butter cookie
*Yogurt:* whisk in cocoa along with honey and vanilla
*Topping:* toasted chopped peanuts and a drizzle of melted chocolate

**Strawberry-Basil Shortcake:**
*Base:* shortbread cookie
*Yogurt:* whisk in strawberry preserves along with honey and vanilla
*Topping:* sliced strawberries and chopped basil leaves

**Fig and Pine Nut Tart:**
*Base:* Italian pignoli (pine nut) cookies
*Yogurt:* whisk in a little balsamic vinegar with extra honey (and omit vanilla)
*Topping:* fresh figs, pine nuts, and a touch of chopped rosemary

**Citrus Coconut Tart:**
*Base:* oatmeal cookie
*Yogurt:* whisk in orange marmalade or lemon curd along with honey (and omit vanilla)
*Topping:* blood orange sections and toasted coconut flakes

*When peaches are in season, and it's a great year for them, my favorite way to eat them is to open wide and take a bite. But if they're less than stellar, or if I overdose on eating them raw, I'll bake them under a blanket of granola. This achieves the same effect as a pan full of bubbling hot fruit crisp—without the leftovers. Depending on the size of the peach and what you had for dinner, half the fruit may be enough to satisfy your sweet tooth, but I'll forgive you if you scarf down the whole peach. Adding a scoop of ice cream, of course, takes this deliciously over the top.*

# ONE-PEACH CRISP with CARDAMOM and HONEY

Preheat the oven to 350°F.

Put the peach halves, cut sides up, in a small baking dish. Drizzle with 1 teaspoon of the honey and sprinkle with the cardamom.

If the granola includes dried fruit, pick out the fruit pieces and reserve them. Pack the granola onto the peach halves. If your granola isn't on the sweet side, feel free to drizzle on the remaining 1 teaspoon of honey.

Bake the peach until it is soft when you pierce it with a fork, about 20 to 25 minutes. Remove from the oven, let cool for a few minutes, then sprinkle with the dried fruit reserved from the granola. Add the scoop of ice cream and eat it while it's warm.

1 **large ripe peach, halved and pitted**

1 **to 2 teaspoons honey**

1/8 **teaspoon ground cardamom**

1/3 **cup Almond and Coconut Granola with Ginger and Cherries (page 160) or other granola, preferably one with nuts and dried fruit**

**Ice cream**

*Perhaps it's not wise, but I judge relationship potential by how a guy eats. That is, a man who consumes food with gusto stands a better chance with me than one who pokes around at his plate, complains about (large) portion sizes, or declares dessert off-limits. When I met Carl, he had a few dietary quirks (no cooked fruit!), but a healthy appetite otherwise. A few months into our dating, he wasn't feeling so well one night, so I made a chicken soup with ginger and green onions. It perked him up so completely that a half hour after finishing it, he smiled and said, "Got any cookies?" I didn't, but couldn't pass up the opportunity to bake something from scratch. I was in the process of moving, and anxious to get rid of the last bits of pantry items, so I took a basic chocolate chip cookie recipe and started subbing various things in and out, keeping proportions the same but adding a little coconut, some oats, some pecans. I tipped in a little splash of a favorite secret ingredient: Fiori di Sicilia, a vanilla-orange elixir from Italy. A half hour later, Carl's eyes widened as he bit into one. "What is that flavor that tastes a little bit of citrus, a little vanilla?" he asked. "Nice palate," I responded nonchalantly, awarding him serious points. Then he uttered the favorite words of every cook I know: "Can I have another one?"*

# CARL'S CHOCOLATE-CHUNK COOKIES

### MAKES 8 TO 10 VERY LARGE COOKIES

Sprinkle the pecans into a small skillet over medium-high heat. Cook, shaking the pan frequently, until the nuts start to brown and become fragrant, a few minutes. Immediately transfer them to a plate to cool; if you leave them to cool in the pan, they can burn. Once they are cool, chop them.

Preheat the oven to 350°F. In a mixing bowl, whisk together the all-purpose and whole wheat flours, oats, coconut, baking soda, and salt. In a separate small bowl, using an electric hand mixer on medium-high, beat the butter and sugar until fluffy. Beat in the egg and Fiori di Sicilia.

Reduce the mixer speed to low, add the flour mixture, and mix just until incorporated. Stir in the chocolate chunks and pecans. Line two baking sheets with parchment paper. Drop 1/4-cup mounds of dough onto the sheets, 4 inches apart.

1/2 **cup raw unsalted pecan halves**

1/2 **cup all-purpose flour**

1/4 **cup whole wheat flour**

1/4 **cup rolled oats**

2 **tablespoons unsweetened finely shredded coconut**

1 **teaspoon baking soda**

1 **teaspoon salt**

8 **tablespoons unsalted butter, softened**

3/4 **cup packed light brown sugar**

1 **egg**

1 **teaspoon Fiori di Sicilia or vanilla extract, or 1/2 teaspoon orange oil plus 1/2 teaspoon vanilla extract (optional)**

6 **ounces bittersweet chocolate, shaved with a knife into irregular slivers and chunks**

continued >

Bake, rotating the sheets halfway through, until golden brown on the edges, 12 to 15 minutes. Remove the cookies and let them cool on the baking sheets. The cookies can be stored in an airtight container at room temperature for up to three days.

NOTE: You can freeze these before baking. Just drop the mounds onto just one baking sheet, as close together as you need without touching, and freeze them until firm. Then transfer them to heavy-duty freezer bags and store in the freezer for up to six months. To bake from frozen, increase the time to 25 minutes or longer.

*I get wide-eyed and foolishly deep-pocketed at a good farmers' market, and old habits die hard. That's why even though my sister and brother-in-law's blueberries were starting to come in strong, I couldn't help but buy the entire stash of wild ones sold by Chick Farm at the North Berwick, Maine, market the first time I tasted them. (My apologies to the customers behind me.) Once I got them home, the race was on to use them—an enviable problem, I realize. This smoothie was one of the first things I made, and it stuck around, for obvious reasons. I like a smoothie in the morning when it's too hot to think about eggs and toast, or, of course, after a workout, or as a midafternoon snack. Obviously, you can shift around the ingredients to suit your taste or to match the seasons, but in my book, it's not a smoothie without a banana (or an avocado if you're going the savory route) to make things silky. I like my smoothies on the thick side, which is what you get with these proportions; if you want something thinner you can use regular yogurt or splash in a little milk or juice. For more smoothie ideas, see page 137.*

# BLUEBERRY GINGER SMOOTHIE

Puree all the ingredients except the honey in a blender until frothy and smooth. Taste, add honey if you'd like things to be sweeter, and blend again to combine.

1 banana

1/2 cup blueberries, stemmed

1/2 cup plain whole-milk Greek-style yogurt (may substitute low-fat or nonfat Greek-style yogurt or regular yogurt)

1 tablespoon chopped fresh ginger

4 fresh mint leaves

4 ice cubes

1 teaspoon or more honey (optional)

# More Smoothie Ideas

Smoothies might be the ultimate in mix-and-match cooking, especially for the single cook, because you can throw in things you like and with a blur of the blender blades they all come together. My caveat is that, as always, you must taste and adjust the seasonings to your liking, especially the honey since much of the balance depends on the sweetness of the fruit you're starting with. Except for the tomato-kale-avocado smoothie, these begin with the base recipe of 1 banana, $1/2$ cup Greek-style yogurt, and 4 ice cubes, which you puree with the rest of the ingredients in a blender.

**Cherry-Almond:** $1/2$ cup pitted sweet cherries, 2 tablespoons roasted unsalted almonds, pinch of cardamom, and 1 teaspoon honey

**Plum-Pomegranate:** 2 or 3 pitted and chopped red or black plums, 1 tablespoon pomegranate molasses, and 4 mint leaves

**Apple-Walnut:** 1 cored and sliced Granny Smith apple, 2 tablespoons toasted walnut halves, pinch of cinnamon, 1 tablespoon lemon juice, and 1 teaspoon honey

**Tomato-Kale-Avocado:** $1/2$ cup Greek-style yogurt, 4 ice cubes, $1/4$ cup stripped and chopped kale leaves, $1/2$ pint stemmed and halved cherry tomatoes, $1/2$ avocado, 1 tablespoon lime juice, and 1 teaspoon honey

*The discovery of this jam was a happy result of clean-out-the-fridge fervor. Blueberries at the farmers' market demanded to be bought, and cried out to be made into jam. I also had on hand some mulled red wine syrup (a recipe that I include in Serve Yourself), and I needed to make space in my crowded refrigerator. So one went into the other. Instead of making the fully spiced version of that syrup (something I suggest for leftover wine—even combinations of different wines from a dinner party), you can start with the most important three ingredients: wine, sugar, and vanilla. This deeply flavored jam has much less sugar than most, so for safety's sake I recommend making a small batch and storing it in the refrigerator, where it will last for a few months, rather than canning it. The jam can also be frozen for up to 1 year. Use it on toast, in yogurt, or to make impromptu individual fruit tarts by baking 1/4 cup or so on a small sheet of store-bought all-butter puff pastry.*

# BLUEBERRY WINE REFRIGERATOR JAM

### MAKES 1 TO 1¹/₂ PINTS

In a large saucepan over high heat, combine the wine and sugar. Cut the vanilla bean in half and scrape the seeds in, then add the pod halves. Cook until reduced by two-thirds and syrupy, about 10 minutes. Fish out the pods and discard (or let them dry and add to a jar of sugar to perfume it for future uses). Stir in the blueberries.

Reduce the heat to medium and cook, stirring occasionally, until the blueberries break down, then taste and add a little more sugar if desired. Cook until the mixture thickens, about 20 to 30 minutes. Spoon into sterilized half-pint jars, screw on lids, and let cool, then store in the refrigerator or freezer.

1 bottle full-bodied red wine, such as Grenache, Syrah, or Cabernet

1 cup sugar, plus more to taste

1 vanilla bean

2 pounds (about 1¹/₂ quarts) blueberries, cleaned and stemmed

# THE VEGETARIAN RESTAURANT GROWS UP

Food is not a chore; it's a gift.

—**ANNA THOMAS**, *The New Vegetarian Epicure*, 1996

Despite the name, Mother's Cafe in Austin served food that was nothing like my mother's. My mother blanketed her meatloaf with cream of mushroom soup, combined an already-cooked broccoli head with a stick of butter and a package of cream cheese before baking it in a casserole, and concocted "Texas salad" with a head of iceberg lettuce, a block of cheddar cheese, a bag of Fritos, a can of pinto beans, and a bottle of tomato-red Catalina dressing. At Mother's, when I started going there in the mid-1980s, cooks were rolling tofu into tortillas for enchiladas, layering lasagna noodles with spinach and ricotta, tossing spinach salad with sunflower sprouts and other raw vegetables, and drizzling it with a cashew-tamari dressing. To this poor college student, Mother's was a welcome respite from the Top Ramen and beans-and-rice bowls I was making at home.

Mother's was my first vegetarian dining experience, and even though I wouldn't have dreamed of becoming vegetarian back then, I never felt out of place there. I craved the food

not because it was meatless, but because it was satisfying every time.

But let's be clear: as much as I loved Mother's, it was certifiably ambition-free. The food was good, yes, but if the menu ever changed, I sure don't remember it. The only sign of progress came when a fire forced renovations, and when they started bottling and selling that salad dressing. Aside from that, in most ways Mother's has been stuck in time, and in Austin, birthplace of the "Keep [Insert Hip City Name Here] Weird" movement, it can get away with it.

Not too many other places can, not in my book anyway. I've had more than my fill of "veggie sandwiches" that consisted of leaden bread, overripe avocado, bland tomato, and a good inch or so of tightly packed bean sprouts that tasted like so much hay. Or menus filled with quotation marks that signaled their dependence on mock meat rather than, well, vegetables. Especially at places with higher ambitions than diner-style comfort food or juice-bar takeout, my disappointments became frequent enough to keep me away altogether. Even once I started eating less and less meat, I tended to cook vegetable-focused meals for myself rather than risk ordering them out. Every now and then I would succumb, and something or other would remind me of what I wasn't missing. Just last year on a trip to San Francisco, it was a soggy pizza at the iconic Greens, the restaurant that started the whole vegetarian-fine-dining thing back in 1979, and a tasteless mélange of mushrooms and polenta at the stylish Millennium Restaurant in the Hotel California. The East Coast has been the location of some vegetarian disappointments, too, most recently a kale salad at the vaunted Candle Café in Manhattan that seemed as if it had been sitting around the walk-in for a day or two too long.

The experiences left me deflated, especially since I've had such memorable, innovative vegetable dishes in both cities. In San Francisco, there were bergamot-glazed beets with mint and flowers at Coi; asparagus cooked in butter with sesame, grapefruit, and fennel at Manresa; a salad of cauliflower, bitter turnip, and crispy kale dressed in a preserved lemon and caper vinaigrette at Flour + Water. In New York, I tasted the most beautiful mushroom consommé of my life at Dan Barber's Blue Hill. And on the Upper West Side, Dovetail's meatless Monday menu is a thing of beauty, full of clarified flavors and inventive treatments. But those are all nonvegetarian restaurants, which got me wondering: Do vegetarian restaurants operate on a different standard? Do they slack off, perhaps, because they have a captive audience of people who, because of the dearth of vegetarian places, will come to one no matter

what? Do omnivorous restaurants, by contrast, try harder to please? Or is there something fundamentally different about the vegetarian palate that I just wasn't getting?

I never made it to Ubuntu, the Napa Valley restaurant that earned Jeremy Fox and then Aaron London such kudos, but knowing that Fox wasn't a vegetarian himself made me ask another question: whether it's a matter of palate or experience or something else altogether, does it take an omnivorous chef to make outstanding vegetarian food?

My curiosity was piqued, and I wanted some answers. Meanwhile, some trends were giving me hope. Savvy restaurateurs have long known that they could capitalize on the growing number of vegetarian diners by catering to them. The farm-to-table movement has had many chefs rediscovering the beauty of vegetables, too, applying at least as much creativity to preparing them as they do to meat. Surely these two trends would start to merge, and if they already had, then maybe some of the newer vegetarian restaurants I started hearing about might represent a welcome evolution.

Any restaurant that would name itself Dirt Candy must have a sense of humor. And as soon as a friend and I squeezed in for a 10 p.m. reservation (the only one we could score a couple weeks out) at this eighteen-seat place on New York's Lower East Side, we were feeling it. That's partly because the staff members' energy was infectious as they danced around one another in the cramped space, but also because we got such a kick out of reading the menu. Carrot buns? Fried cauliflower and waffles? Popcorn pudding? Yes, please.

Our favorite: the Asian-style steamed buns made with the juice of three different varieties (and colors) of carrot, with caramelized carrots inside instead of the usual pork belly.

Turns out that one of those energetic staff members was owner Amanda Cohen herself, and when we asked her how she comes up with her dishes, she smiled mischievously and shrugged. "I just have crazy ideas," she said. The story is energetically told in her new cookbook, also called *Dirt Candy*, which in a move that suits her personality perfectly, is illustrated comic book–style. After all, this is someone whose website proclaims, "Anyone can cook a hamburger, but leave the vegetables to the professionals."

When I called Cohen later, she said she started Dirt Candy with one straightforward mission: to be the vegetarian restaurant she had long wanted to go to. When she would eat out at omnivorous places, she said, "I would think, 'I cannot believe this is what you're serving as a vegetarian entrée.'" And vegetarian spots seemed completely unaffected by the larger, more exciting restaurant scene: "There were just so many things going on in cooking that just weren't showing up at these places in any way."

She agrees that one reason for the lack of creativity might be the built-in audience, but she sees it changing. "When I opened Dirt Candy, I was so lucky. I knew I could coast for a couple of months because every vegetarian person in the city would come and see what I was doing. So yes, there's this group that you didn't have to maybe try so hard for. But I do think that nowadays, you have to try a little harder."

I ask her if she thinks the fact that she's not vegetarian anymore—she describes herself as pescetarian—better positions her to cook for them. Her answer: definitely. "It's not that you have less baggage, it's that you have more tools to work with," she said. "I'd probably be an even better chef if I ate meat. It's very hard to understand, if you eat vegetables all your life, what a meat eater wants to eat. For people who eat fish and chicken and beef and pork, flavor is different. They want something saltier and greasier and juicier. If I give them a raw carrot salad, I understand why they wouldn't want to eat it unless they're on a diet."

Speaking of raw carrots, Cohen used to work at Pure Food and Wine, which caused a sensation in New York when it opened in 2004 to serve something more common on the West Coast: raw food. The tenets of raw food hold that heating anything above 118°F destroys important vitamins, minerals, and enzymes. I don't know that I buy the philosophy, but all of that felt beside the point when my friend and I slid into the sleek, dark dining room near Union Square. The food would speak for itself.

When it did, it wasn't as playful as the food at Dirt Candy, but it had its moments. I've seen lasagna made of zucchini ribbons before, but other dishes surprised us. A crunchy, spicy, fresh Philly roll combined avocado, kimchi, and a faux cheese made of cashews. The pistachio topping on a portobello mushroom dish tasted as pungent and funky as if it had blue cheese in it. Miniature mushroom tacos were so deconstructed we couldn't quite tell what was going on, possibly because we gobbled them before we had a chance to analyze.

Near us, a loud table gathered for a birthday celebration seemed segregated by gender, and the female side was in a better mood than the male. As the women took pictures and everybody clinked glasses of sangria, one of the guys shouted out: "Next year we're going to Atlantic City!" Why? "Because there are no vegan restaurants in Atlantic City." Ba-dum-dum.

I felt a pang of sympathy for two women staffing the host station just a few feet away, but I'm sure they've heard it all before. On our way out, I tried to make up for our neighbors by praising the food. "Which was your favorite?" one asked.

"The Philly roll," I said.

"Oh, I love that one," she replied, "especially with that *cream cheese*." And she winked when she said "cheese," and I returned the gesture when I said, "Yes, that's really good *cheese*." And there we stood, winking at each other as if vegan food required some kind of code.

In an age where some of the biggest food trends involve things that our grandparents took for granted, everything old is new again. That is why I was so curious to try Kajitsu. Well, that and the fact that Momofuku's pork-worshipping chef, David Chang, included this—a vegan place, no less!—on his list of places to eat in 2012.

Just down the street from Dirt Candy but at the opposite end of the spectrum, cooks at Kajitsu celebrate the ancient Buddhist tradition of *shojin* cooking, which is by its nature vegetarian. My friend and I raced there in separate cabs through rainy traffic, frazzled and almost twenty minutes late for our reservation, but the smell of cedar incense and the minimal space's earth-toned decor immediately set us at ease. The word *kajitsu* means "fine day," and we soon forgot about the not-so-fine weather outside.

In true Japanese style, as much attention was paid to the dishware as the food, with stunning pieces of pottery—some of it quite old—chosen to complement the carefully cooked and arranged ingredients. In keeping with Buddhist tradition, any chipped pottery was repaired rather than discarded—an ancient idea perfectly suited to modern tastes. But the artistic commitment didn't stop there. Take the dish our waitress announced as "spring vegetables": it was a cherry leaf fried on just one end to look like frost, covering up a nest of brussels sprouts, asparagus, zucchini, and oyster mushrooms. The dish that made us a little dizzy was a matte white square bowl filled with a bright green pea broth and a single quarter of a fennel bulb, super soft but with caramelized, slightly chewy edges, along with a few sparsely placed snap peas, sansho pepper flower, and little rolls of yuba, the creamy skin formed when making fresh tofu. I'm not sure whether much of this would be considered that innovative in Tokyo, but in Manhattan it was revelatory.

The next-best taste came at the tail end of the run. The new chef, Ryota Ueshima, fresh from Japan, had "prepared a special course to celebrate his first day," our waitress announced: apple chunks topped with plum jelly. Tart and sweet, simple yet amazing. And yet we couldn't help imagining a decidedly nonvegan application: it would be so perfect on ice cream.

When I told colleagues at a food conference last year that I was researching the topic of vegetarian dining, more than one of them mentioned Vedge, which Rich Landau and Kate Jacoby opened in the fall of 2011 in Philadelphia after many years of running the acclaimed Horizons. Actually, "mentioned" is the wrong word. They insisted I get there. An imperative. So I followed orders, and headed to Philly on a hot summer weekend.

As I sat waiting for a friend, chatting with the easy-on-the-eyes waiter, and sipping the Elder Sage cocktail—gin, St. Germain, lemon, grapefruit bitters, and sage—I was overtaken by one thought. With off-white walls, dark wood trim and flattering lighting in its collection of rooms, the place seemed like, well, a normal restaurant, as silly as that may sound.

I took a look at the menu, and I was immediately hooked. Every dish spoke my language; these were my favorite things to eat and my favorite ways to eat them. There were seasonal vegetables of all stripes, of course, but it was the preparations and accompaniments that really got me: the nouns included kimchi, sambal, fennel pollen, gochujang, salsa verde, remoulade, romesco, and black vinegar, and the verbs included pickled, smoked, charred, cured, grilled, toasted, and roasted. I started to regret inviting only one friend, because I wanted one—or more—of everything.

Just listen to the sound of these: roasted white eggplant with togarashi barbecue and smoked miso mayo. Asparagus and roasted rutabaga salad with charred onion and pistachio vinaigrette. Lemongrass corn bisque with pickled chile and napa cabbage. They tasted as good as they sounded. A cold cucumber avocado soup had the perfect balance of bracing high notes from cilantro and mint anchored by the lightest touch of earthy cumin and smoked *pepitas*. Mushroom carpaccio was tart from pickled cabbage and cornichons but tickled the back of the throat with a healthy dose of fresh horseradish. The pleasures didn't stop at dessert, either: we dug into gold Rainier cherries over a silky custard sprinkled with toasted coconut flakes.

Simply put, Landau and Jacoby put forth the most exciting vegetarian food I've ever tasted. Actually, the food is vegan, something that was pretty easy to forget. Why? I think it's because in Landau's cooking, nothing is trying to be something else. No sleight of hand, no need to pay-no-attention-to-the-man-behind-the-curtain. This was honest food. Every ingredient played its role, and its role was to help the starring vegetable shine.

Perhaps it was partly because they were small plates rather than traditional entrées, but the dishes seemed so complete, so satisfying, and not one of them called attention to the fact that it didn't include animal products. I couldn't stop thinking about this for days. If someone had brought me to Vedge without telling me anything about it, and I just tasted the food, I think it would have taken me a while before I realized that there was no meat—or even dairy—in anything. If had I tasted those foods blind, it would have been even harder. And that's not because anything tasted like meat, or fish, or eggs. It's that I didn't miss the animal elements at all; I was too busy enjoying everything else.

When I talked to Landau at the restaurant that night, he said something that stuck with me: "Vegetarian is a diet. Vegetables are food." That's why you don't see the former word used in any of the restaurant's marketing materials, something Vedge has in common with Dirt Candy. In a later conversation, Landau and Jacoby said such terminology has been key in their goal to blow up the mold of a vegetarian or vegan restaurant. "We wanted to distinguish ourselves from the places where they had just been smoking pot and the Grateful Dead was playing, and they were stirring the vegetarian chili with a wooden spoon," Landau said. "We wanted to stand up there with the Vetris and the Zahavs of Philly, rather than the veggie cheesesteak joint down the street. So we had to drop the word *vegan*. You don't have to advertise what the dietary limitations might be. We want to be a vegetable restaurant."

Do places like Vedge and Dirt Candy represent the future of vegetarian dining? Perhaps. As restaurant consultant Clark Wolf told me, "If we can have eight million steakhouses, we can have a few places that properly gather and prepare vegetables wonderfully," he said, then chuckled. "For God's sake, as a culture, we need the roughage, on so many levels." Still, he thinks we'll eventually move past all that, to a point where appreciation of vegetables is so widespread the labels aren't needed. Fewer of his clients are saying that they want to start a vegetarian or vegan restaurant, but vegetables are playing a larger part in every project he comes across. "I've been recently working on a wine bar concept in Greenwich Village, and there are so many vegetable items on the menu," he said. "Not because we want to fill a slot but because the chef is young and modern, and he knows what he wants to cook and eat."

Sounds like a smart guy. I'll bet he knows something else I have noticed about this style of dining, something too important for me not to mention. After a long night of indulging in large quantities of meat, I usually feel anything but fabulous, but the night I was at Vedge couldn't have been more different. This wasn't spa cuisine by a long shot, yet even though my friend and I plowed through a good portion of the menu, and I had several glasses of wine after a cocktail, I floated out feeling blissful and satisfied, somehow energized and lightened by the experience rather than weighed down by it. And later, I drifted off to sleep dreaming of an open field, a table snaking through it, and vegetables spilling over, as far as the eye could see.

## Chapter 6

# ENTERTAINING

I t may seem obvious, but just in case it's not, let me say for the record: cooking for one and cooking for others aren't mutually exclusive. The fact that I love making interesting dinners for myself on weeknights when I'm alone doesn't do anything to detract from my urge to make larger-scale, sometimes more ambitious dinners—or brunches, or cocktail party nibbles—for friends on the weekend. If anything, every now and again I get a true hankering to pull out the stops—and my biggest pans—and cook for a crowd.

This is not a cookbook about entertaining. There are plenty of those. But I couldn't resist pulling together a few of my favorite recipes for party appetizers, especially since many of them double as condiments I keep on hand to use in other recipes. Not only does that mean I can find an easy use for party leftovers, but it also works the other way around. One night with friends, it's a spicy-salty poblano tapenade dip we scoop up with tortilla chips; the next day, that same dip becomes a sandwich spread. If I've got a few of these condiments/dips stored in my refrigerator, I'm a party just waiting to happen. What are you doing tonight?

*I'm in love with the combination of kimchi and eggs, and these came to me when I was look-ing for a flashy appetizer to take to an author event at the Smithsonian. But they became a standby in Maine when I had abundant access to fresh eggs but no one in the house to share them with, since my sister and brother-in-law had decided to go vegan. This recipe depends on the use of good kimchi, so either make the Cabbage Kimchi (page 163) or buy the best you can find, probably at an Asian market. These can be refrigerated, covered, for up to 2 days, but are best eaten within a few hours of being made.*

# KIMCHI DEVILED EGGS

### MAKES 1 DOZEN

Prick each egg just barely through the shell on the rounded end, using an egg pricker or a thumbtack.

Bring a medium saucepan full of water to a boil. Reduce the heat so that the water is at a simmer. Use a slotted spoon to carefully lower each egg into the water and to stir them frequently for the first minute or so of cooking. (This helps set the yolks in the center.)

Meanwhile, pour 4 cups of water into a large bowl and stir in 1 or 2 cups of ice.

Cook the eggs for 11 minutes, then transfer them to the ice water. As soon as you can handle the eggs, reach into the water and crack them all over, keeping them in the water. Remove them one at a time and remove a large piece of the shell at the rounded end, where an air pocket should be, then return them to the water. (This helps water get between the egg and the shell for easier peeling.) Remove one egg at a time, slip off the rest of the shell, and return it to the water as you continue peeling.

Transfer the peeled eggs to a countertop, and slice each one lengthwise in half. Pop out each yolk half with your fingers into the bowl of a food processor or blender, and set each white on a serving platter.

Drain and gently squeeze the kimchi of its liquid and finely chop it. Add ½ cup of the kimchi and all the cream cheese to the food processor or blender and puree until smooth. Taste,

6   eggs, preferably at least a week old, at room temperature

¾   cup Cabbage Kimchi (page 163) or highest-quality store-bought kimchi, preferably spicy

¼   cup cream cheese

Sea salt

Sriracha

continued  >

add salt as needed, and add Sriracha a little at a time if you want it to be spicier.

Use a teaspoon to carefully fill each egg white half with the kimchi mixture, mounding it on top. (Or, if you want to be fancy, spoon the filling into a pastry bag fitted with a decorative tip, or a plastic ziplock bag with one corner cut off, and pipe it onto each egg white half.) Finely chop the remaining 1/4 cup of kimchi and sprinkle it on top of the eggs. Squirt a few drops of Sriracha on each egg.

Refrigerate the stuffed eggs for at least 1 hour, covered, so the cream cheese firms up, and serve.

*Can you guess what this is, in a Brangelina or Bennifer kind of way? What if I called it kim-amole? Yep, that's it, a marriage of kimchi and guacamole. This isn't anything close to traditional, but it's what happened when I was called upon to make a quick appetizer for a group of hungry people while I was staying in an unfamiliar house, and these ingredients were staring me in the face. The most important thing is to not mash the avocados the way you would when making the real thing, so they stay delightfully chunky. The second most important thing is to not tell your guests what it is until they taste it. Trust me; it's more fun that way.*

# GUACA-CHI

## SERVES 4 AS AN APPETIZER

In a serving bowl, toss the avocado chunks with the lime juice. Chop the kimchi if the pieces are bigger than bite-size, and gently toss it and all its liquid with the avocado. Taste, add salt if necessary, and serve with tortilla chips or crackers.

- Flesh of 1 ripe avocado, cut into large chunks
- 2 tablespoons freshly squeezed lime juice (from 1 lime)
- 1/2 cup Cabbage Kimchi (page 163) or store-bought kimchi, preferably spicy, with its liquid
- Sea salt

*Walnuts give this eggplant dip more body than the classic Middle Eastern treatment, baba ghanoush, and the addition of dates (or figs plus honey) and vinegar take it into sweet-and-sour territory. Eat with pita chips, or use as a topping for Chickpea Pancake with Broccoli and Eggplant Puree (page 82).*

# OTTOMAN EGGPLANT DIP

### MAKES ABOUT 1 CUP

Preheat the oven to 500°F. Prick the eggplant with a fork in several places, transfer to a baking sheet, and roast until it collapses, 40 to 50 minutes. Remove, and let it cool.

While the eggplant is roasting, sprinkle the walnuts into a skillet over medium-high heat. Cook, shaking the pan frequently, until the nuts start to brown and become fragrant, a few minutes. Immediately transfer them to a plate to cool; if you leave them to cool in the pan, they can burn.

When the eggplant is cool enough to handle, slice it open and scrape the flesh from the skin into the bowl of a food processor. You should have about ¾ cup. Add the dates, vinegar, paprika, walnuts, garlic, and salt and process until smooth. Taste and add more vinegar and salt as needed. Store in the refrigerator in an airtight container for up to 1 week.

1 medium Italian eggplant (about 12 ounces)

⅓ cup raw walnut halves

2 large Medjool dates, pitted and chopped, or 3 dried Mission figs, chopped, plus 1 teaspoon honey

1 tablespoon red wine vinegar, plus more to taste

½ teaspoon smoked Spanish paprika (pimentón)

1 clove garlic, chopped

½ teaspoon sea salt, plus more to taste

*I'm not sure why it took me so long to steer tapenade toward Mexico, given my palate. But I did, inspired by the fact that I needed to use up a couple of poblano chiles while they were still fresh and quickly not getting any fresher. The result is a sharp little condiment that I immediately added to my regular rotation. Spread it on sandwiches (such as the Tofu, Grilled Cabbage, and Poblano Tapenade Sandwich on page 49), use it to add a little zip to pasta sauce, scoop it onto halved hard-cooked eggs (or mix it with the yolks for devilish fun), smear it on steamed potatoes, scoop it up with crudités, plop it inside tacos. Heck, use it on everything. You'll see.*

# POBLANO TAPENADE

## MAKES ABOUT 1½ CUPS

Turn the oven broiler on high. Place the poblanos on a shallow rimmed baking pan and put it on one of the racks set so that the poblanos are as close to the broiler as possible without touching. Broil the poblanos until the skin has blistered and slightly charred all over, turning them as they brown. Transfer them to a bowl, cover it with a plate, and let them steam.

Soak the capers in a small cup of cold water for a few minutes, then rinse and squeeze them dry.

When the poblanos are cool enough to handle, slip off the charred skin and discard it. Remove and discard the stems and seeds and drop the poblanos into the bowl of a food processor. Add the capers, olives, garlic, anchovy, ancho chile powder, olive oil, and lime juice. Pulse until you have a chunky paste; it might seem too loose, but it will firm up in the refrigerator. Taste and add salt if needed. (If you used the anchovy, you probably won't need any salt.)

Use what you want immediately, then transfer the rest to a small glass jar, screw on the lid, and refrigerate for up to 2 weeks.

8 ounces poblano chiles (2 to 3 medium chiles)

1 tablespoon capers, preferably salt-packed

½ cup pitted green olives

2 cloves garlic, peeled and smashed

1 anchovy fillet (optional)

¼ teaspoon ancho chile powder

3 tablespoons extra-virgin olive oil

1 tablespoon freshly squeezed lime juice (from ½ lime)

Sea salt (optional)

*Serve this to friends, of course, or hoard it for yourself and spread it on sandwiches, or use in Potato and Bean Tostadas (page 113). Any variety of bean works well in this recipe, but chickpeas, pintos, and cannellinis are my favorites.*

# SMOKY BEAN and ROASTED GARLIC DIP

### MAKES ABOUT 1¹/₂ CUPS

Preheat the oven to 375°F. Place the garlic cloves on a sheet of aluminum foil, drizzle lightly with olive oil, and fold up the foil tightly. Bake until the cloves are very tender, about 20 minutes. Let cool slightly.

When the garlic is cool enough to handle, squeeze the tender cloves from their peels into the bowl of a food processor. Add the beans, ¹/₄ teaspoon of the paprika, and the vinegar and pulse until combined. With the machine running, add the bean cooking liquid a tablespoon or two at a time and continue processing until the dip is thin enough to easily spread or dip a chip into, but not runny. Taste and add salt as needed, plus another ¹/₄ teaspoon or more of the paprika if you want it smokier.

If you're not serving immediately, transfer to a small jar, pour olive oil on top to cover, cover with an airtight lid, and refrigerate for up to 2 weeks, or freeze in a small ziplock bag (see "A Vacuum Shortcut," page 171) for up to 6 months.

6 cloves garlic, unpeeled

1 tablespoon olive oil, plus more for storage

1¹/₄ cups cooked beans, preferably homemade, rinsed if canned, and drained

¹/₄ to ¹/₂ teaspoon hot Spanish smoked paprika (pimentón picante)

1 teaspoon apple cider vinegar

Bean cooking liquid or water

Sea salt

*Whenever I get my hands on good ricotta (or when I make my own), the first thing I want to do is to whip—really, puree—it with my favorite olive oil and a little salt, turning it silky smooth. If the ricotta and olive oil themselves are delicious, the combination is killer, but it also takes well to many spices; my favorite additions are smoked salt, smoked Spanish paprika (pimentón), ground cumin, fresh oregano leaves, or za'atar (page 169). This makes a fabulous dip with breadsticks or crackers, a topping for bruschetta (by itself or under slow-roasted tomatoes, red pepper chutney, or tapenade), or a condiment for sandwiches such as the Ricotta, Zucchini, and Radicchio Sandwich on page 52.*

# WHIPPED RICOTTA

## MAKES ABOUT 1 CUP

Combine the ricotta and olive oil in the bowl of a small food processor or blender and puree until smooth. Taste, add salt as needed, and puree again until combined. Use immediately, or transfer to a covered container and refrigerate for up to 5 days.

1 cup highest-quality ricotta, preferably full fat

2 tablespoons highest-quality extra-virgin olive oil

Sea salt

# THE POLITICS OF COOKING

EXCERPTED AND ADAPTED FROM A MAY 2011
SPEECH AT THE CLINTON SCHOOL OF PUBLIC SERVICE
IN LITTLE ROCK, ARKANSAS

I started moving toward food journalism more than a dozen years ago because I found myself tiring of news. But guess what's happened in the intervening years? Food is news, big news. And it turns out that I wasn't really tiring of news. I just felt the need to combine my passion and my journalistic calling into one, more specific vocation. Since then I've been happy to be able to be in a position at the *Washington Post* to help direct coverage of food and food news and to have a role, however small, in shaping an increasingly important debate. You have no doubt heard some of the statistics. I'll start with the most dramatic, something I found so shocking the first time I heard it: we have given birth to what experts say could very well be the first generation of Americans who probably will not outlive their parents. Another one: we waste 40 percent of the food that we buy. And, finally: nearly one in four children in America struggles with hunger.

Crucial debates are happening right now about how to address some of these issues and others. One of the most important questions

is whether the local food movement is elitist, whether it bypasses low-income people. And then there's the following question, which I find particularly provocative: is industrial agriculture, which depends on the use of pesticides, genetic modification, and other technological "advances," really best suited, as its proponents say, to solve world hunger because of the efficiency that those advances afford?

These are difficult questions, and God knows I don't have the answers to them, but I have met—and read the work of—people who I think have figured some of it out. That elitism charge is a complicated one, but groups like Wholesome Wave, among others, are helping answer it through programs such as one that lets food-stamp recipients double their spending power at farmers' markets. And when it comes to that industrial agricultural question, I'm going to share with you a quote from someone who I think addresses it beautifully. I was recently involved with a conference that the *Post* organized at Georgetown University called "The Future of Food," and I had the pleasure of sitting next to the great poet, farmer, and essayist Wendell Berry, whose speech was just about what you would expect from a great poet, farmer, and essayist.

Here's what he said: "There is no use in saying that if we can invent the nuclear bomb and fly to the moon, we can solve hunger and related problems of land use. Epic feats of engineering require only a few brilliant technicians and a lot of money. But feeding a world of people year to year for a long time requires cultures of husbandry fitted to the nature of millions of unique small places. Precisely the kind of cultures that industrialism has devalued, uprooted, and destroyed."

I cannot put things as succinctly or as poetically as Wendell Berry, but I do have some strong beliefs about food. The foremost one is this: I believe that the crucial link between you and your health, the health of your family—whether you have one now or you plan to build one later—and, in fact, the health of the planet is cooking. Food is cheaper if you cook it yourself and you know how to do it in a way that's not wasteful. Food is more sustainable if you make the choice to buy it from farmers who grow it in a way that respects the land—or, of course, if you grow it yourself in such a manner—but you have to know what to do with it when you bring it home. If you learn to eat seasonally, if you get in the habit of preserving food at the peak of harvest and doling it out to yourself and your family over the course of the winter when it's not so plentiful, food is not just cheaper, it is more delicious and it is more nutritious.

As students, you may not have families yet, but most of you eventually will, and I believe that you're not going to able to take care of them in a way that's healthful and nourishing unless you first practice on someone else. Now who might that someone else be? There's an irony here. How do you tell students in a school of public service that the most important thing is to serve themselves? I like to think of it this way: you know that safety instruction speech that the flight attendant makes on the airplane? The message includes talk of the oxygen masks dropping from the ceiling, and always ends with something like this: "Please secure your own mask before helping others." At this point, the video or the diagram pretty much always shows a mother and a child.

As a kid I was horrified by that last instruction. Shouldn't the mother take care of the comparatively helpless child first? It took me many years before I understood. If the mother or father or any caretaker doesn't guarantee her or his own safety first, she or he risks not being able to take care of anybody else.

True selflessness is not a sustainable quality in a parent, and in my opinion it's really not a sustainable quality in anyone who's trying to be a good citizen. And the analogy extends perfectly to what I want to say to you about cooking. How are you going to be healthy enough to contribute to the world in whatever way you decide to contribute—whether it's raising a family, writing a book, working on a political campaign, working for a nonprofit—if you don't know how to take care of yourself? Food is not just about deliciousness; as delicious as it can be, it is also about nourishment. And only when you know how to nourish yourself can you commit to nourishing others.

One of the things I want to do with my books and my column is to show people that it is important and self-sustaining and healthy and responsible to learn how to cook for yourself. But more than that. Not only is it possible to overcome the obstacles of shopping—portion size, leftovers, storage (don't get me started on celery)—but it can actually be fun. For instance, I love throwing dinner parties. I love sharing the fabled pleasures of the table with friends and family that I cook for, but isn't there always a little bit of performance anxiety involved? I have a good friend who will never make for company something he hasn't taken on a "dry run" first.

But when it's "just you," when you're, as the food writer Laurie Colwin put it, "alone in the kitchen with an eggplant"—which sounds a little dirty, I know—there is no performance anxiety. There's no dry run. You follow your cravings wherever they may take you. You can improv to your heart's content, and if things don't work out, the worst thing that's going to happen is it's not going to taste very good. And if you don't want to eat it, you don't have to eat it, and that's the day that you can ring up your local pizza place. You can try again another time, and there's nobody there to judge you for it.

For me, cooking is positively meditative, and I wish that it were that way for everybody, but I know that it's not. When I get off work at the end of a long day, I am often what I refer to as "hangry," a mash-up of "hungry" and "angry." It's that state of being when you are having a hard time processing information because you haven't eaten—or more than that, it's when the lack of food has made you positively irritable. I think my doctor might refer to it as low blood sugar, but I think "hangry" has a better ring to it. Whatever you call it, it's dangerous, because when I'm hangry and I'm presented with immediate access to food, my judgment goes out the window. But if I have planned well enough, the hangriness doesn't get the best of me because I have the means to satisfy myself with healthy food. I start thinking on my walk home about what's in my pantry, what's in my fridge, what's in my freezer, what combinations I have that I might be able to put together, especially without going to the store.

I'm thinking: Do I still have some of that kimchi that I made a few weeks ago? Do I have rice in the freezer from the Chinese take-out I got last week? Do I have a head of cauliflower sitting in my "rotter"? (That's what I call the crisper because of what happens to things I put in there.) If I have those things, I know I can make a really great fried rice dish. Do I have eggs? Do I have that red pepper chutney I made the other day? Do I have a bag of potato chips and frozen shrimp? I've got the makings of a Spanish-style tortilla. You get the idea.

There are more than 31 million of us living alone in the United States now. It's the fastest-growing household demographic in the country and it has been for twenty years. There are enough of us that you think there would have been scores of cookbooks on the subject by now. We make up more than a quarter of all homes, and the reason for the growth of the demographic is three-pronged. On one end, it's young people who are waiting longer and longer to get married. It used to be that you would move from Mom and Dad's house to college to your spouse's house. Now the window between parents' and spouse's house is larger and larger, and more people are foregoing the spouse's house altogether. On the other side of the demographic, older people who outlived their spouses are able to live longer independently. Someone who is used to cooking for a husband and family now is having to adjust to the idea of cooking for one. In the middle are the divorced people, or people who were living with someone but aren't anymore because the relationship ended.

I think what those 31 million people need to figure out, if they haven't already, is that when the pressure changes and the oxygen level in their world drops, and they find themselves hungry and tired and maybe a little angry about it, something is available to help them. When the oxygen mask drops down, that mask represents cooking. Cooking can relieve not just the hunger, but the pressure. And we need to be able to put that mask on our own faces first, and breathe.

## Chapter 7

# RECIPES for the FRIDGE, FREEZER, and PANTRY

Time for a little math lesson. Take the number of servings in your average recipe, subtract one, and you've got the number of leftover meals that await the single cook who makes it. We single folks make a recipe that serves four, and we have three meals' worth of leftovers. Couples make the same, and they have just one to get through. Leftovers don't seem so problematic at first, but the feeling fades. When I take leftover lasagna to work the day after I had it for dinner, I feel proud of myself; when I face it that night, I'm not too excited. The day after that? I'm beleaguered.

Instead, I like to think of almost everything I make as the building blocks of a future meal. So rather than make a vat of black bean chili and freeze it for countless meals later, I make just the black beans and refrigerate or freeze them, and then add them to this or that as the week goes on. On most weekends, I make a pot of brown rice, or I braise a load of greens, or I marinate and bake a batch of tofu, or I simmer another variety of beans to velvety perfection, or I make a batch of spicy tomato sauce. Some weekends I do more than one. The goal: to make the path from fridge to plate as short as possible.

When I tasted the amazing granola at Charleston's Hominy Grill, I had a revelation: there isn't so much of a difference between the kind of granola I like the best and one of my favorite sweets, the oatmeal cookie. It was a liberating moment, because it meant I could stop thinking about granola as a health food and could therefore stop being upset when I read nutritional labels that surprised me with the amount of fat included. Now that I think of granola instead as a rich, indulgent snack, I eat much less of it. Oh, who am I kidding? I scarf it down as quickly as I do an oatmeal cookie. You will, too. By the way, it's worth seeking out both sizes of unsweetened coconut: the smaller works its way throughout the granola and gives coconutty background, while the larger provides chewier, more noticeable bits here and there. I like the brand Let's Do Organic, sold in natural foods stores. Also, feel free to use this as a template to make your own favorite granola. Ingredients to mix and match include: sweeteners (maple syrup, agave nectar), oils (coconut, olive), extracts (vanilla, coconut), nuts (pistachios, pecans), grains (quinoa, wheat germ) and dried fruit (cranberries, apricots).

# ALMOND and COCONUT GRANOLA with GINGER and CHERRIES

**MAKES ABOUT 6 CUPS, OR TWELVE 1/2-CUP SERVINGS**

Preheat the oven to 375°F.

In a large bowl, combine the oats, almonds, and finely shredded coconut, mixing thoroughly. Transfer to a large, heavy baking sheet and bake, stirring occasionally, until the mixture is golden and toasted, 15 to 20 minutes.

Meanwhile, in the same bowl, whisk together the oil, honey, almond extract, and salt. Stir in the large coconut flakes and the crystallized ginger.

When the oat mixture is toasted, remove it from the oven and pour it back into the bowl and stir to thoroughly coat it with the honey mixture.

Line the baking sheet with parchment paper and return the granola mixture to it. Spread it out, packing it lightly with a spatula. Bake until the granola is browned at the edges but still pale toward the center of the pan, 10 to 15 minutes, then use the spatula to scoop it up, stir, and again pack it lightly. Continue baking until the granola is fragrant and deeply browned, 10 to 15 minutes.

| | |
|---|---|
| 3 | cups rolled oats |
| 1 | cup slivered or sliced almonds |
| 1/2 | cup finely shredded unsweetened coconut |
| 1/4 | cup canola or other neutral vegetable oil |
| 3/4 | cup honey |
| 2 | teaspoons almond extract |
| 1 | teaspoon sea salt |
| 1/2 | cup large unsweetened coconut flakes |
| 1/4 | cup finely chopped crystallized ginger |
| 1 | cup unsweetened dried cherries |

continued >

< Almond and Coconut Granola with Ginger and Cherries, continued

Remove from the oven, and let the granola cool completely before removing it from the pan. It will crisp as it cools. Break up the granola and toss it with the dried cherries. Store it in an airtight container, preferably in a cool, dark place, for up to 2 weeks.

NOTE: If you want it to stay extra-crisp, store the granola and the dried cherries separately, and combine them for each serving.

**Use granola in:**

**One-Peach Crisp with Cardamom and Honey (page 132)**

### TIP

Use a $1/4$-cup dry measuring cup to measure both the canola oil and the honey. First, fill it with the canola oil, then pour the oil into the bowl. Then, without rinsing the cup, pour the honey into it three times, pouring it into the bowl each time. Because the cup is oiled, the honey will slide right out.

*This is a slight simplification of the kimchi recipe in Serve Yourself, in that I'm leaving out the Asian pear (which does add a nice little note of sweetness). Why? Well, I seem to find myself with all the other ingredients around, even when Asian pears are out of season or otherwise hard to find, and I love the kimchi without it. As always, make sure to seek out the real Korean chile flakes, which makes a real difference. Strict vegetarians, use 4 teaspoons of red miso instead of the oyster and fish sauces to approximate that funky depth.*

# CABBAGE KIMCHI

### MAKES ABOUT 4 CUPS

Toss the cabbage with the salt in a large bowl. Let it sit until it exudes liquid and wilts, 60 to 90 minutes. Lift the cabbage out of the excess liquid by the handful, squeeze it dry, and transfer it to another bowl, discarding the liquid. Do not rinse the cabbage.

Combine the chile flakes, garlic, ginger, water, sugar, oyster sauce, and fish sauce in the bowl of a food processor. Process until smooth, scraping down the sides of the bowl if needed.

Add to the cabbage mixture, tossing to combine, and let sit, covered, at room temperature overnight, then transfer to an airtight container and move to the refrigerator. Wait at least a few days before using the kimchi, which will get more pungent as the days go by and is at its best for about a month, although you can eat it for longer if you like it really funky (which I do).

- 1 head napa cabbage (1$^1$/$_2$ to 2 pounds), cored and cut into 2-inch pieces
- 1 tablespoon kosher salt
- $^1$/$_4$ cup Korean red chile flakes
- 6 cloves garlic, peeled
- 1 (2-inch) piece fresh ginger, peeled and chopped
- 2 tablespoons water
- 2 teaspoons sugar
- 2 teaspoons oyster sauce (optional)
- 2 teaspoons fish sauce (optional)

**Use kimchi in:**

Cold Spicy Ramen Noodles with Tofu and Kimchi (page 18)

Grilled Kimcheese (page 45)

Guaca-chi (page 148)

Kimchi Deviled Eggs (page 146)

Sweet Potato, Kimchi, and Greens Hash (page 108)

*Be prepared for a revelation: you probably would never think to put a cabbage on the grill, but you should. Besides adding smoky flavor, grilling brings out the vegetable's natural sweetness, making it appealing even for people who didn't think they liked cabbage. Grilled cabbage is an easy accompaniment to grilled meats, particularly pork, or it can be the basis for a twist on your favorite coleslaw recipe. This will be easier if you have a grill basket, but it's doable without it. The cabbage can be grilled, then cooled to room temperature and refrigerated in an airtight container for up to 1 week.*

# GRILLED CABBAGE

## MAKES ABOUT 6 CUPS

Olive oil

1 medium green or red cabbage (about 2½ pounds)

Sea salt

Freshly ground black pepper

Prepare the grill for direct heat. If using a gas grill, preheat to medium-high (450°F) and add soaked wood chips in a foil packet or in a smoker box. If using a charcoal grill, light the charcoal or wood briquettes; when the briquettes are ready, distribute them under the cooking area for direct heat. For a medium-hot fire, you should be able to hold your hand about 6 inches above the coals for 4 or 5 seconds. Have ready a spray bottle filled with water for taming any flames. Lightly coat the grill rack with oil and place it on the grill.

Cut the cabbage in half, top to bottom, slicing through the core. Cut each half into 1-inch-thick slabs, leaving the core intact as much as possible. Brush both sides of the slabs with oil, using 3 to 4 tablespoons in all, and sprinkle generously with salt.

Using a grill basket if you have one, grill the cabbage slabs until they are charred in spots on the outside and starting to wilt (but not soft) on the inside. (If some of the leaves come loose and start to burn, use tongs to pull them off and transfer them to a plate while you cook the remaining cabbage.)

Transfer the cooked slabs to a cutting board; cut out and discard the core. Cut the grilled leaves into thin slices.

If serving as a side dish, season with more salt and pepper to taste.

**Use grilled cabbage in:**

Roasted Sweet Potato, Japanese-Style (page 87)

Smoky Cabbage and Noodles with Glazed Tempeh (page 27)

Tofu, Grilled Cabbage, and Poblano Tapenade Sandwich (page 49)

*I make these every so often and use them on pizza and in quesadillas and other dishes. The timing here is quite variable, depending on the sugar content of the onions, their freshness, the size of the pan, and other factors. One thing is for sure: you will start out with what seems like a lot of sliced onions, and you will end up with what seems like not very much, so if you can think of lots of immediate uses for them, feel free to double or triple this recipe. Keep in mind that when they're done right, they're packed with flavor and jammy-sweet, so you don't need much.*

# CARAMELIZED ONIONS

## MAKES ABOUT 1/2 CUP

Toss the onion slices in a medium bowl with the salt. Set aside until they exude liquid, at least 30 minutes and up to 2 hours. Drain the onions, reserving the liquid. Squeeze the onions by the handful, removing as much of the liquid as possible, and reserve the liquid.

Pour the olive oil into a large skillet over medium heat. When it starts to shimmer, add the onions. Cook, stirring or tossing often, until the onions collapse and start to brown; this could happen as quickly as 10 or 15 minutes, or take twice that long. Reduce the heat to low, add the liquid from the bowl, and pack the onions down in the pan with a spatula. Cook them very slowly, scraping the pan of browned bits and tossing the onions once every 10 minutes or so. They will be slightly browner every time you toss them. Continue doing this until the browning accelerates, then start scraping and tossing more frequently until the onions are very soft, deeply browned—the color of dark caramel, as it turns out—and sweet. It could take an hour or more to get there, but it's worth it.

Refrigerate the onions in an airtight container for up to 1 week, or freeze them in ice cube trays, then transfer to ziplock bags (see "A Vacuum Shortcut," page 171) and freeze for up to 6 months.

1 pound yellow or white onions (about 3 medium onions), thinly sliced

1/2 teaspoon kosher salt

2 tablespoons extra-virgin olive oil

**Use caramelized onions in:**

**Chicken-Fried Cauliflower with Miso-Onion Gravy (page 109)**

**Kale and Caramelized Onion Quesadilla (page 54)**

**More Savory Tart Ideas (page 80)**

**Oyster Mushroom and Corn Tart (page 79)**

*This is my favorite marriage of techniques gathered over many years of cooking eggs. If you are cooking more than one egg, use a saucepan large enough to fit them all without crowding, plus an even larger ice bath. Note that the timing here is for an egg that you are going to eat plain or use as a topping, and for that purpose I like it to be slightly soft and creamy in the very center. If you are scooping out the yolks to make deviled or stuffed eggs, or otherwise want to cook the yolks all the way through, add a minute to the cooking time. Whatever you do, don't go any longer than that, or you'll risk the telltale sign of an overcooked egg: a green ring around the yolk. Feel free to multiply this recipe, of course, and to keep hard-cooked eggs around for up to a week in the fridge. Note that I prefer using older eggs for this; fresh-from-the-chicken eggs are notoriously difficult to peel.*

# PERFECTLY CREAMY HARD-COOKED EGG

Prick the egg just barely through the shell on the rounded end, using a clean egg pricker (a little tool made for just this use) or a thumbtack.

Bring a small saucepan full of water to a boil. Reduce heat so that the water is at a simmer. Use a slotted spoon to carefully lower the egg into the water, and stir it frequently for the first minute or so of cooking. (This helps set the yolk in the center.) Meanwhile, pour 2 cups of water into a large bowl and stir in a cup or so of ice.

Cook the egg for 9 minutes for a yolk that's still a little soft in the very center, or 10 minutes for one that's barely cooked through, then transfer it to the ice water. As soon as you can handle the egg, reach into the water and crack it all over, keeping it in the water. Remove a large piece of the shell at the rounded end, where an air pocket should be. (This helps water get between the egg and the shell to get peeling started more easily.) Slip off the rest of the shell, transfer the peeled egg to a countertop, and use as desired. Store peeled eggs covered with a damp paper towel inside an airtight container, in the refrigerator for up to 1 week.

1 egg, preferably at least a week old, at room temperature

**Use hard-cooked eggs in:**

**Enfrijoladas with Egg, Avocado, and Onion (page 110)**

**Kale and Mango Niçoise Salad (page 22)**

**Kimchi Deviled Eggs (page 146)**

*Some chile oils pack such a punch you can only use a few drops at a time. I prefer to make mine a little milder, but you can vary the amount of red pepper flakes to suit your taste. You can achieve slightly different effects by using Korean chile flakes or, if you can find them, crushed chipotle flakes for an extra smoky oil.*

# CHILE OIL

### MAKES 1 CUP

Pour the oil into a small skillet over medium-high heat. When it starts to shimmer, turn off the heat, sprinkle in the red pepper flakes, and let the oil cool to room temperature. Pour it through a strainer into a small glass jar and screw on the lid. It will keep for months at room temperature.

1 cup vegetable, peanut, or sesame oil

1 tablespoon crushed red pepper flakes

**Use chile oil in:**

**Cold Spicy Ramen Noodles with Tofu and Kimchi (page 18)**

**Lemon Chile Vinaigrette (page 26)**

**Spicy Kale Salad with Miso-Mushroom Omelet (page 24)**

*Like curry, za'atar is a spice blend that varies from cook to cook in the Middle East, its birth-place. My father was Assyrian, so I've always enjoyed the flavors of the region (though the closest I've yet traveled is Turkey). This is my interpretation, and it reflects my priorities: my favorite part of za'atar is the tart sumac, so it's particularly heavy in my version. And while some cooks grind their spices together, I like to leave the sesame seeds whole. You can find sumac in Middle Eastern groceries and from online sources such as Penzeys and Kalustyan's. For a perfect, quick snack, combine with olive oil and brush on pita.*

# ZA'ATAR

### MAKES ABOUT ½ CUP

Put the sesame seeds in a small dry skillet over medium heat. Toast the seeds, tossing the pan occasionally, until they become fragrant and start to lightly brown. Immediately transfer them to a bowl to cool; if you leave them to cool in the pan, they could burn.

Stir in the sumac, thyme, cumin, and salt. Transfer to a small jar with a lid and store in a cool, dark place for up to 6 months.

1 tablespoon sesame seeds
¼ cup sumac
2 tablespoons dried thyme
1 tablespoon ground cumin
1 teaspoon sea salt

**Use za'atar in:**

Cheesy Greens and Rice Gratin (page 75)

Pomegranate-Glazed Eggplant (page 91)

Tomato and Feta Tart (page 80)

Whipped Ricotta (page 153)

*This is my favorite way to eat tofu—well, other than that amazing freshly made, softly set, custardy stuff you can get throughout Asia and in some Asian restaurants in the States. For the firm tofu that's the easiest to come by here, I like to gently press out some of the extra liquid to make it a little more absorbent, then marinate it overnight, sprinkle on some cornstarch, and bake it until the edges are crispy and the inside is still a little creamy. Then I can keep it around for a week and throw it into dishes here and there, leaving it cold for salads and heating it up again in things like stir-fries, where it holds its shape better than fresh tofu.*

# MARINATED and BAKED TOFU

**MAKES ABOUT 4 CUPS**

Wrap the drained tofu in paper towels, place on a plate, place a second plate on top of the tofu and put a large unopened can of tomatoes or beans on top; let the tofu exude liquid for about 30 minutes. Unwrap the tofu and pat it dry. Cut the tofu into 1-inch cubes.

In a gallon-sized plastic ziplock bag, combine the sesame oil, soy sauce, rice wine or sherry, vinegar, garlic, ginger, water, and Sriracha. Massage the bag to combine the ingredients. Add the tofu cubes and gently toss to combine, then seal the bag according to the instructions on page 171. Refrigerate for at least 2 hours, or as long as overnight, turning the bag over a couple of times. (Alternatively, you can marinate the tofu in a glass or stainless steel bowl and cover it for refrigeration, opening and tossing it a time or two while it's marinating.)

Preheat the oven to 350°F.

Drain the tofu, reserving the marinade (see Note), and transfer the tofu to a large bowl. Use a fine-mesh strainer to sprinkle the cornstarch onto the tofu a little at a time, gently turning the tofu in the bowl to coat it between each addition.

Line a baking sheet with parchment paper, and transfer the tofu to the baking sheet. Bake the tofu until it is crisp and lightly browned, turning it every 15 minutes or so, for about 45 minutes total.

2 **pounds firm or extra-firm tofu, drained**

2 **tablespoons toasted sesame oil**

2 **tablespoons soy sauce**

2 **tablespoons rice wine or sherry**

2 **tablespoons rice vinegar, preferably unseasoned, or apple cider vinegar**

2 **cloves garlic, finely chopped**

1 **(2-inch) piece fresh ginger, peeled and grated or thinly sliced**

¹/₄ **cup water**

1 **teaspoon Sriracha or your favorite Asian hot chile paste**

2 **tablespoons cornstarch**

2 **teaspoons sea salt**

Serve or eat some or all of the tofu immediately either on its own or in a recipe, or cool and refrigerate in an airtight container for up to 1 week.

NOTE: If desired, reduce the marinade into a glaze to use for a batch of this tofu or as a dipping sauce for vegetables, or to drizzle on Indonesian Tofu and Egg Wraps (page 55). To do that, pour it into a large skillet over high heat and cook until it is as thick as gravy and reduced, about 10 minutes.

**Use tofu in:**

Cold Spicy Ramen Noodles with Tofu and Kimchi (page 18)

Cool, Spicy Mango Yogurt Soup (page 57)

Indonesian Tofu and Egg Wraps (page 55)

Roasted Sweet Potato with Southeast Asian Topping (page 87)

Spicy Basil Tofu Fried Rice (page 106)

Szechuan-Style Tofu and Shiitake Stir-Fry (page 115)

Thai-Style Kabocha Squash and Tofu Curry (page 117)

Tofu, Grilled Cabbage, and Poblano Tapenade Sandwich (page 49)

Tomato-Braised Green Beans and New Potatoes (page 118)

## A Vacuum Shortcut

Foods freeze better when they're not just airtight, but vacuum-sealed to prevent freezer burn. Systems like the FoodSaver line use heavy-duty plastic bags and a motorized vacuum to suck the extra air out of them, and then heat-seal them. It's a great system, but if you're only freezing things in ziplock bags every so often, or if you're working on a shorter-term job, such as marinating, there's a much lower-tech solution. It doesn't result in as perfect a seal, but it's surprisingly close. Here's what you do:

Pour the food you want to vacuum-seal into the bag. Press to almost completely seal the bag, but leave an inch or so unsealed at one end to let air escape.

Find a bowl that's slightly bigger in volume and height than the ziplock bag with water, and put it in the sink. Slowly immerse the bag in the water, watching to make sure you don't let water into the bag. The water will push air up and out of the bag as you lower. Try to get the surface of the water as close to the bag's top edge as possible without immersing, then carefully press to complete the seal, and remove the bag.

*I'll make it brief: this is the only way I like raisins. And I like these a lot. Put them on salads, puree them with mayonnaise for a sandwich condiment, whisk them into store-bought salsa verde for a salad dressing, spoon them over roasted or grilled asparagus, potatoes, eggplant, and other vegetables, or serve them at a party on a cheese and pickle tray.*

# QUICK-PICKLED GOLDEN RAISINS

## MAKES ABOUT ¹/₂ CUP

Put the raisins in a pint jar.

Combine the vinegar, sugar, and crushed red pepper in a small saucepan over medium-high heat. Bring to a boil, turn off the heat, and pour over the raisins. Let cool to room temperature, then cover and refrigerate the raisins in their liquid for up to 2 months.

¹/₂  cup golden raisins

¹/₂  cup apple cider or white wine vinegar

¹/₄  cup sugar

¹/₂  teaspoon crushed red pepper flakes

**Use quick-pickled golden raisins in:**

Curried Broccoli and Warm Israeli Couscous Salad (page 21)

Curried Mushroom Bean Burgers (page 42)

*I've long been in the habit of cooking ingredients in advance and then using them in dishes. But because greens cook so quickly, I hadn't gone there with them until I read Tamar Adler's gorgeous book,* An Everlasting Meal. *In suggesting this as a habit, she helped me prevent the calamity that was too often occurring when I would buy lovely greens at the farmers' market, only to store them too long in the fridge and help the crisper live up to the alias I've given it: the rotter. This recipe makes use of the stems, too, but if you're in a hurry you can compost some or all of them instead, or freeze them to make vegetable stock (page 59). Omnivores, you may be tempted to add a few slices of bacon to the garlic and onion; Southerners, a ham hock might be calling out to you.*

# HEARTY GREENS

## MAKES 3 TO 4 CUPS OF GREENS IN THEIR LIQUID

Fill your sink with cold water. Strip the greens from their stems, reserving the stems, and drop the leaves into the sink as you work. Let the leaves sit in the water for about 10 minutes, gently swishing them from time to time, so any dirt settles on the bottom of the sink. Scoop them out a few at a time with your hands and transfer them to a large bowl; do not dry them in a salad spinner or otherwise. Coarsely chop them, working in batches if necessary, and return them to the bowl as they are chopped. Rinse the stems and thinly slice them.

Heat the oil in a large Dutch oven or other large pot over medium heat. When it shimmers, add the sliced stems, garlic, and crushed red pepper and sauté until the stems and garlic are barely tender. Add the greens and any water remaining in the bowl. Cook for a few minutes until the greens start to collapse, then use tongs to toss them lightly; cover, and cook until they are tender, about 10 minutes. Stir in the vinegar, taste the result, and add salt as needed.

Use immediately, or let cool at room temperature and store in an airtight container in the refrigerator, greens and liquid together, for up to 1 week. Or freeze in ziplock bags (see "A Vacuum Shortcut," page 171) for up to 6 months.

2¹⁄₂ **pounds hearty cooking greens, such as kale, collards, chard, or beet greens, or a mix**

1 **tablespoon extra-virgin olive oil**

2 **cloves garlic, thinly sliced**

¹⁄₂ **teaspoon crushed red pepper flakes**

¹⁄₄ **cup apple cider vinegar**

**Sea salt**

**Use greens in:**

**Cheesy Greens and Rice Gratin (page 75)**

**Green Gumbo (page 58)**

**Grilled Greens, Chickpea, and Peppadew Sandwich (page 50)**

**Risotto with Greens and Zucchini (page 105)**

**Sweet Potato Galette with Mushrooms and Kale (page 88)**

**Sweet Potato, Kimchi, and Greens Hash (page 108)**

*Especially in the fall and winter, I eat beans, in some form, several times a week. Which means that once every week or two, I put a pot on the stove so I can draw from it for a multitude of recipes. This is my most stripped-down, no-time-for-futzing recipe; it's almost as easy as opening a can, and it results in beans with a far superior taste and texture, without all the sodium of most store-bought canned brands. And if you use dried beans from a company such as Rancho Gordo or from a local farmer, instead of ones from a supermarket that may be years old, you won't believe the difference.*

# POT of BEANS

## MAKES ABOUT 6 CUPS BEANS AND 2 TO 4 CUPS BROTH

Rinse the beans, picking through them to remove any debris. Pour them into a bowl and add enough water to cover them by at least 2 inches. Soak for at least 6 hours and preferably overnight. (Alternatively, do a quick soak. Bring the beans and water to a boil then turn off the heat and let them sit for an hour.)

Drain and rinse the beans, and transfer them to a medium pot set over medium heat. Add enough water to cover them by about 2 inches. Add the onion and garlic. Increase the heat to medium-high and bring to a boil. Reduce the heat to low or medium-low so that the liquid barely simmers, cover, and cook the beans until four or five that you sample are creamy and tender, as little as 45 minutes and as long as 2 hours, or even longer, depending on the variety and age of the beans.

Add the salt and cook for another 10 or 20 minutes so that the beans absorb it. Taste and add more salt if needed.

Cool whatever portion you're not using immediately to room temperature. Refrigerate the beans in their broth in an airtight container for up to 2 weeks, or freeze in ziplock bags (see "A Vacuum Shortcut," page 171) for up to 6 months.

1 pound dried beans of any variety except lentils, fava beans, or field peas

1 small yellow or white onion, cut into 1-inch chunks

2 large cloves garlic, peeled and smashed

2 teaspoons fine sea salt, or more to taste

---

**Use beans in:**

Asian Bean and Barley Salad (page 16)

Bean and Israeli Couscous Soup (page 66)

Bean and Poblano Soup with Cinnamon Croutons (page 63)

Curried Mushroom Bean Burgers (page 42)

Enfrijoladas with Egg, Avocado, and Onion (page 110)

Grilled Greens, Chickpea, and Peppadew Sandwich (page 50)

Potato and Bean Tostadas with Avocado–Green Onion Salsa (page 113)

Roasted Sweet Potato with Southwestern Topping (page 87)

*My go-to tomato sauce, this is what I make periodically just to have around for pasta dishes, baked vegetables, bruschetta, eggs—pretty much anything but dessert. I prefer using whole tomatoes instead of crushed because I like the chunky texture. If you want to use fresh tomatoes, it's best to use a sauce variety such as Roma or San Marzano; first blanch them in boiling water for a minute or two and then slip off the skins.*

# TOMATO SAUCE with a KICK

**MAKES ABOUT 4 CUPS**

Pour the tomatoes into a bowl and use your hands to squeeze and crush them.

Pour the olive oil into a large skillet over medium heat. Add the onion, garlic, anchovies, and oregano and cook until the vegetables soften. Sprinkle in the crushed red pepper (less or more depending on your appetite for spiciness), stir, and cook them for just a few seconds. Add the tomatoes and bring the mixture to a boil.

Reduce the heat slightly so that the sauce is at a vigorous simmer but isn't rapidly boiling. (Use a splatter guard if you have one.) Cook until the sauce is thickened and slightly reduced and the tomato pieces have become very soft, 20 to 30 minutes or longer if desired. (Break them up further with a wooden spoon or potato masher if desired.) Turn off the heat.

Stir in the sugar, vinegar, salt, and a couple of grinds of black pepper. Taste, and add more of any or all of them until the sauce reaches the balance you like.

2 (28-ounce) cans whole tomatoes in their juice (about 6 cups), preferably San Marzano

2 tablespoons extra-virgin olive oil

1 large onion, chopped

4 cloves garlic, chopped

2 anchovies, finely chopped

1 tablespoon dried oregano

1/4 to 1/2 teaspoon crushed red pepper flakes

2 teaspoons sugar, plus more to taste

2 teaspoons red wine vinegar, plus more to taste

Kosher salt

Freshly ground black pepper

**Use tomato sauce in:**

Baby Eggplant Parm (page 74)

Cheesy Greens and Rice Gratin (page 75)

Spinach Enchiladas (page 85)

Steamed Eggplant with Miso-Tomato Sauce (page 114)

Tomato-Braised Green Beans and New Potatoes (page 118)

*I came home with a bag of brown basmati rice from Kalustyan's, one of my favorite purveyors of spices, teas, and staples in New York City, for one reason: the directions on the bag. They promised that I could make this rice by following the most memorable proportion possible— equal parts rice and water—and by cooking it for only 30 minutes, half the time it takes to cook short-grain brown rice. A half hour to cook a whole grain rice? Sold. Now it's my favorite rice variety, and method. While I've seen many other cooking instructions calling for soaking, rinsing, cooking with twice as much water, and cooking much longer, I stopped believing all of them, because this technique works like a charm. And it's so easy, I never have to look it up. This results in a relatively dry rice, with the grains distinct and separated; if you want some- thing with the grains plumper and a little stickier, add another 2 cups of water and cook the rice another 10 to 15 minutes, until the water is fully absorbed, before letting it sit.*

# QUICK POT of BROWN RICE

### MAKES ABOUT 5 CUPS

Rinse the rice under running water, then drain it. Combine the rice, water, and salt in a 2-quart saucepan over medium-high heat. Bring to a boil, then reduce the heat to a simmer, and cover. Cook for 30 minutes, then turn off the heat and let the rice sit, covered, for 15 minutes. Uncover and fluff with a fork.

2 cups brown basmati rice

2 cups water

1 teaspoon kosher salt

**Use brown rice in:**

Asian Bean and Barley Salad
(page 16)

Cheesy Greens and Rice Gratin
(page 75)

Spicy Basil Tofu Fried Rice
(page 106)

Thai-Style Kabocha Squash
and Tofu Curry (page 117)

*What a versatile thing this is to keep in your refrigerator at the height of summer, when your garden—or your farmers' market basket—is overflowing. Eat it as a side dish, toss it (hot) with pasta, or eat it (cold) on salad greens. Or put it in a gratin dish, crack an egg on top and roast in a 400°F oven until the white is set but the yolk remains runny. For the fresh lima beans, you can substitute edamame, another fresh shell bean, or thawed frozen lima beans. Succotash can be refrigerated for up to 1 week or frozen, preferably in cup-size containers, for up to 6 months.*

# SUMMER SUCCOTASH

### MAKES 4 SERVINGS

Heat the oil in a large skillet over medium heat. Once the oil starts to shimmer, add the crushed red pepper flakes and smoked paprika; stir and let sizzle for a few seconds, then add the anchovy, onion, and garlic. Cook, stirring frequently, until the onion and garlic are tender.

Add the lima beans and water; bring to a boil, then reduce the heat to medium-low, so that the water is barely bubbling around the edges. Cover, and cook just until the lima beans are barely tender, about 10 to 15 minutes.

Uncover; add the zucchini and tomatoes, then increase the heat to medium. Cook, stirring occasionally, until the zucchini starts to become tender, just a few minutes, then add the corn kernels and cook just until they brighten in color and start to lose their raw crunch. Remove from the heat. Season with salt to taste.

If you are eating a portion right away (or at room temperature), garnish with 2 chopped basil leaves; wait to add the equivalent of 2 basil leaves to each of the remaining 3 servings until just before they are eaten.

1 tablespoon extra-virgin olive oil

$1/2$ teaspoon crushed red pepper flakes

$1/2$ teaspoon hot Spanish smoked paprika (pimentón picante)

1 anchovy fillet (optional)

1 small onion, chopped

2 cloves garlic, finely chopped

2 cups fresh lima beans

$1/2$ cup water

1 large zucchini, trimmed and cut in half lengthwise, then crosswise into $1/2$-inch slices

2 large tomatoes, cored, then chopped, with their juices

Kernels from 2 ears of fresh corn (see page 180)

Kosher or sea salt

8 large basil leaves, stacked, rolled and cut crosswise into thin slices

## Cutting Corn Kernels

I've seen all sort of gimmicky tricks and tried all manner of gadgets to help cut the kernels off corn cobs, all of them aimed at keeping the pesky buggers from flying all over—and off—the countertop. But my favorite method is pretty simple: just cut the cob in half crosswise first, then stand each half-cob cut-end down before you slide your knife down one side and then repeat all the way around. Not only does the flat end make the cobs more stable for cutting, but since they're shorter, the kernels don't have as far to fall—or fly.

When you're done husking, by the way, save the husks and silks (and the shorn cobs), freezing if necessary. When you have time, put them in a big pot, cover them with water, and simmer for an hour to make a beautifully clear, light golden stock that carries the essence of summer.

# Resources

## South River Miso Company

www.southrivermiso.com

Beautiful miso, traditionally made in Massachusetts.

## Rancho Gordo

www.ranchogordo.com

The California company that got us eating heirloom beans again also sells fantastic chile powders, dried corn products, and herbs and spices.

## Épices de Cru

www.epicesdecru.com

Simply the highest-quality spices I've seen (or smelled, at their store in Montreal) available in one place.

## Fastachi

www.fastachi.com

The best nuts—raw and perfectly roasted—and nut butters you can buy. The dried fruit is fabulous too.

## Kalustyan's

www.kalustyans.com

A huge selection of spices, nuts, teas, grains, and other international products, such as Lebanese pomegranate molasses that includes just one ingredient: pomegranates.

## Lodge Cast-Iron Cookware

www.lodgemfg.com

Regular and preseasoned cast-iron pans, including skillets as small as 6½ inches in diameter, made in America, plus a new line of preseasoned steel pans that rival those made in France.

# Selected Bibliography

*An Alphabet for Gourmets*, M. F. K. Fisher.

*Ancient Grains for Modern Meals*, Maria Speck.

*Asian Tofu*, Andrea Nguyen.

*Baking from My Home to Yours*, Dorie Greenspan.

*Bean by Bean*, Crescent Dragonwagon.

*Canal House Cooking* (series), Christopher Hirsheimer and Melissa Hamilton.

*The Cookbook Library*, Anne Willan.

*Cooking in the Moment*, Andrea Reusing.

*The Cuisines of Mexico*, Diana Kennedy.

*Entertaining for a Veggie Planet*, Didi Emmons.

*An Everlasting Meal*, Tamar Adler.

*The Food and Wine of Spain*, Penelope Casas.

*Food in Good Season*, Betty Fussell.

*The Gift of Southern Cooking*, Edna Lewis and Scott Peacock.

*The Good Egg*, Marie Simmons.

*The Heart of the Artichoke*, David Tanis.

*How to Cook a Wolf*, M. F. K. Fisher.

*Kansha*, Elizabeth Andoh.

*Mastering the Art of Chinese Cooking*, Eileen Yin-Fei Lo.

*The Meat Lover's Meatless Cookbook*, Kim O'Donnel.

*Mediterranean Greens and Grains*, Paula Wolfert.

*The Mediterranean Kitchen*, Joyce Goldstein.

*Plenty*, Yotam Ottolenghi.

*Ready for Dessert*, David Lebovitz.

*The Southern Foodways Alliance Community Cookbook*, Edited by Sara Roahen and John T. Edge.

*The Sunset Cookbook*, Edited by Margo True.

*Tender*, Nigel Slater.

*Vegetables*, James Peterson.

*Vegetarian Cooking for Everyone*, Deborah Madison.

# About the Author

JOE YONAN is author of *Serve Yourself: Nightly Adventures in Cooking for One* (Ten Speed Press, 2011), which *Serious Eats*, the *San Francisco Chronicle*, and blogger David Lebovitz named one of their favorite books of the year. The book was an outgrowth of his monthly column, Cooking for One, for *The Washington Post*, where he is Food and Travel editor.

Before working at the *Post*, Joe was a food writer and Travel editor at *The Boston Globe*. His writing for the *Post* and the *Globe* has appeared in multiple editions of the Best Food Writing anthology, and he has won awards from the James Beard Foundation for best newspaper food section, the Society of American Travel Writers for best large-circulation newspaper travel section, and from the Association of Food Journalists for his Cooking for One column.

Born in Georgia and raised in West Texas, he got the cooking bug from his Indiana-born mother, who let him shop for the family groceries starting at age 8 and indulged his demands to use her stand mixer because he thought it was so cool. He spent 2012 living with his sister and brother-in-law in southern Maine to learn about (and help with) their homestead, where they are trying to grow as much of their food as possible.

Joe holds a professional chef's diploma from the Cambridge School of Culinary Arts outside Boston and a bachelor of journalism from the University of Texas at Austin. He lives in Washington, DC.

Author photograph by Sarah Gillingham-Ryan

# Index

# Measurement Conversion Charts

## Volume

| U.S. | IMPERIAL | METRIC |
|---|---|---|
| 1 tablespoon | $1/2$ fl oz | 15 ml |
| 2 tablespoons | 1 fl oz | 30 ml |
| $1/4$ cup | 2 fl oz | 60 ml |
| $1/3$ cup | 3 fl oz | 90 ml |
| $1/2$ cup | 4 fl oz | 120 ml |
| $2/3$ cup | 5 fl oz ($1/4$ pint) | 150 ml |
| $3/4$ cup | 6 fl oz | 180 ml |
| 1 cup | 8 fl oz ($1/3$ pint) | 240 ml |
| $1^1/4$ cups | 10 fl oz ($1/2$ pint) | 300 ml |
| 2 cups (1 pint) | 16 fl oz ($2/3$ pint) | 480 ml |
| $2^1/2$ cups | 20 fl oz (1 pint) | 600 ml |
| 1 quart | 32 fl oz ($1^2/3$ pints) | 1 l |

## Temperature

| FAHRENHEIT | CELSIUS/GAS MARK |
|---|---|
| 250°F | 120°C/gas mark $1/2$ |
| 275°F | 135°C/gas mark 1 |
| 300°F | 150°C/gas mark 2 |
| 325°F | 160°C/gas mark 3 |
| 350°F | 180 or 175°C/gas mark 4 |
| 375°F | 190°C/gas mark 5 |
| 400°F | 200°C/gas mark 6 |
| 425°F | 220°C/gas mark 7 |
| 450°F | 230°C/gas mark 8 |
| 475°F | 245°C/gas mark 9 |
| 500°F | 260°C |

## Length

| INCH | METRIC |
|---|---|
| $1/4$ inch | 6 mm |
| $1/2$ inch | 1.25 cm |
| $3/4$ inch | 2 cm |
| 1 inch | 2.5 cm |
| 6 inches ($1/2$ foot) | 15 cm |
| 12 inches (1 foot) | 30 cm |

## Weight

| U.S./IMPERIAL | METRIC |
|---|---|
| $1/2$ oz | 15 g |
| 1 oz | 30 g |
| 2 oz | 60 g |
| $1/4$ lb | 115 g |
| $1/3$ lb | 150 g |
| $1/2$ lb | 225 g |
| $3/4$ lb | 350 g |
| 1 lb | 450 g |

Copyright © 2013 by Joe Yonan
Photographs copyright © 2013 by Matt Armendariz,
except for the temple garden photographs on pages 120–123 which are by Joe Yonan

All rights reserved.
Published in the United States by Ten Speed Press,
an imprint of the Crown Publishing Group, a division of Random House, Inc., New York.
www.crownpublishing.com
www.tenspeed.com

Ten Speed Press and the Ten Speed Press colophon are registered trademarks of Random House, Inc.

Some of the content featured in this book originally appeared in the column
Cooking for One by Joe Yonan, and is reprinted here courtesy of *The Washington Post*.

Library of Congress Cataloging-in-Publication Data

Yonan, Joe.
Eat your vegetables : bold recipes for the single cook / Joe Yonan.
pages cm
1. Cooking (Vegetables)  2. Cooking for one.  I. Title.
TX801.Y66 2013
641.6'5—dc23
2012046939

Hardcover ISBN: 978-1-60774-442-9
eBook ISBN: 978-1-60774-443-6

Printed in China

Design by Toni Tajima
Food styling by Adam Pearson

10 9 8 7 6 5 4 3 2 1

First Edition